HISTORIC ■ SCOTLAND

NEOLITHIC AND BRONZE AGE SCOTLAND

HISTORIC  SCOTLAND

NEOLITHIC AND BRONZE AGE SCOTLAND

P.J. ASHMORE

B. T. Batsford Ltd / Historic Scotland

© P. J. Ashmore 1996
First published 1996

All rights reserved. No part of this
publication may be reproduced, in any form
or by any means, without permission from
the Publisher and Historic Scotland.

Typeset by Bernard Cavender Design & Greenwood Graphics Publishing
and printed in Great Britain by The Bath Press, Bath

Published by B. T. Batsford Ltd
4 Fitzhardinge Street, London W1H 0AH

A CIP catalogue record for this book is
available from the British Library

ISBN 0 7134 7530 7 (cased)
0 7134 7531 5 (limp)

Contents

Illustrations

Colour plates

Acknowledgements

This book is based on the work of many people, some professional archaeologists and others unpaid – all amateurs of archaeology in the best sense. I am grateful to (in alphabetical order) Ian Armit, Fionna Ashmore, John Barber, Gordon Barclay, David Breeze, Marion Fry, Gordon Maxwell, Rod McCullagh, Colin Richards, Anna Ritchie, Graham Ritchie, Jim Rideout, Alan Saville, Alison Sheridan, John Terry and Camilla Toulmin for (sometimes unpublished) information, comments and discussion, and Alan Braby and Chris Unwin for illustrations.

The following individuals and institutions provided, and in most cases hold the copyright for, the illustrations: A. Braby (**29, 33**); the British Museum (**11**); J. Hedges (**74**); Historic Scotland (**3, 4, 5, 6, 7, 8, 9, 10, 13, 14, 20, 21, 23, 25, 26, 34, 35, 37, 39, 40, 42, 43, 48, 51, 52, 58, 59, 61, 62, 63, 64, 65, 67, 68, 69, 72, 77, 82, 83, 84**); D. Hogg (**42**); G. Jobey (**45**); L. Masters (**16**); R. McCulagh; the Trustees of the National Museums of Scotland (**15, 31, 49, 53, 54, 70, 85**); M. O'Neil (**38**); C. Renfrew (**27**); E. Rennie (**18**); A. Ritchie (**22**); the Royal Commission on the Ancient and Historical Monuments of Scotland (**1, 2, 12, 19, 24, 27, 28, 30, 44, 46, 47, 50, 56, 57, 66, 73, 76, 79, 80, 81**); D. Simpson (**71**); Society of Antiquaries of Scotland; Alastair Whittle (**36**). The remaining illustrations were drawn by the author based on original material from D. Simpson (**41**); C. Burgess (**55**); G. Barclay (**60**); E. Carter (**75**) and J. Rideout (**78**).

Introduction

These remains are tanquam Tabulata Naufragy [like fragments of a shipwreck] that after the Revolution of so many Years and Governments have escaped the Teeth of Time and (which is more dangerous) the Hands of mistaken Zeale. So that the retriving of these forgotten Things from Oblivion in some sort resembles the Art of a Conjurer

(John Aubrey, writing in the mid-seventeenth century)

In 1648 that great gossip John Aubrey discovered something extraordinary as he took part in a hunt and 'the Chase led us (at length) through the village of Aubury [Avebury], into the closes there: where I was wonderfully surprised at the sight of those vast stones, of which I had never heard before; as also at the mighty Banke and graffe [ditch] about it. I observed in the Inclosures some segments of rude circles, made with these stones; whence I concluded, they had been in old time complete ... It is very strange that so eminent an Antiquitie should lye so long unregarded by our Chorographers.'

Where others had observed rough stones, his mind built ancient temples; where children had run up and down familiar banks and ditches, he saw the boundary of an ancient and sacred place.

Garnering the evidence

In visiting the great monuments beloved of tourists, and walking above the margins of neatly cultivated fields, or even reading old accounts of monuments we thought we knew well, we sometimes capture the same excitement that Aubrey felt three and a half centuries ago. I felt that excitement in seeing a set of lightly inscribed triangles among the illustrations in James Farrer's book about the Viking runes in Maes Howe; and then finding that ancient carving, made 4000 years before the Norsemen broke into the tomb, unblemished on the great monolith buttressing the south-west corner of the burial chamber (**colour plate 1**).

Such almost random discoveries, arising in the course of work or leisure, have their own delight. Meticulous regional surveys, on the other hand, provide a concentrated burst of discoveries, a breathing of life into things long known but little understood and a gust of understanding into forgotten landscapes. A recent survey of north-east Perth, for instance, has revealed rich overlapping patterns of ancient land use (**1**).

In the lowlands, agriculture has cut away the upper levels of most monuments, but air photography, at the right time of the year, can show up their ditches, pits and post-holes with startling clarity, because they retain moisture which allows the plants to stay green longer.

1 *Houses, fields and burial cairns of the second millennium and later survive at Corrie Burn, and elsewhere in north-east Perth, eastern Scotland, untouched by modern cultivation. Excavation of a double-walled house, like that in the middle of this air photograph, at Carn Dubh (78) revealed that it dated to between about 1400 and 1100.*

now recognize as the remains of a house of continental type set up over 5500 years ago. Along with other bits and bobs left by the people who built it were chance inclusions of charred seeds and potsherds; and with that evidence we can begin to build a picture of how people lived and died.

But for those interested in our past the digging up of pits and potsherds is not the only joy. The world of the laboratory and of the informed imagination beckons. Those

Thus, dramatically and over a period of a few minutes, came the discovery of the great timber hall at Balbridie on Deeside (2). Painstaking excavation revealed sets of post-holes which we

discoloured volumes of soil and fragments of baked clay tell us of a land peopled by strangers, our ancestors, in whose old places we can sense the spirits of those whose eyes looked on our country three hundred generations ago, whose hands broke the old forest, and whose feet walked the first tilled fields. Where the land is not too acid, their bones and those of the animals they hunted and herded contain the stilled twist of life. In lake sediments, in peat bogs and in buried soils beneath the plough-wash filling the ancient hollows of the land, we can find pollen, telling us of hazel thickets and herbs, pastures and fields. Through the microscope, too, we can detect the gradual but incessant changes to the earth, the slow chemical corrosions and the castings of worms which blur and veil the evidence of the past.

The mundane activities of ancient people often influence what those who study ancient environments discover. For instance, lake sediments build up faster when the land around them has been disturbed by agriculture. Cattle penned in an enclosure will enrich the soils beneath them, leaving higher traces of phosphates than in surrounding areas. The pollen found in successive layers in peat bogs and sediments reflects both local and more distant vegetation. If cereal pollen suddenly appears in the layers after a drop in tree pollen, it seems possible that the activities of farmers have changed the local environment. However, it is

2 *At Balbridie, in north-eastern Scotland, a large timber hall dating to about 3600 was discovered by air photography. Most of the ripening crop was light yellow; but the soil in the ancient post-holes retained moisture and the crop above them stayed dark green. The other marks on the photograph reveal relatively recent cultivation, and variations in the geology.*

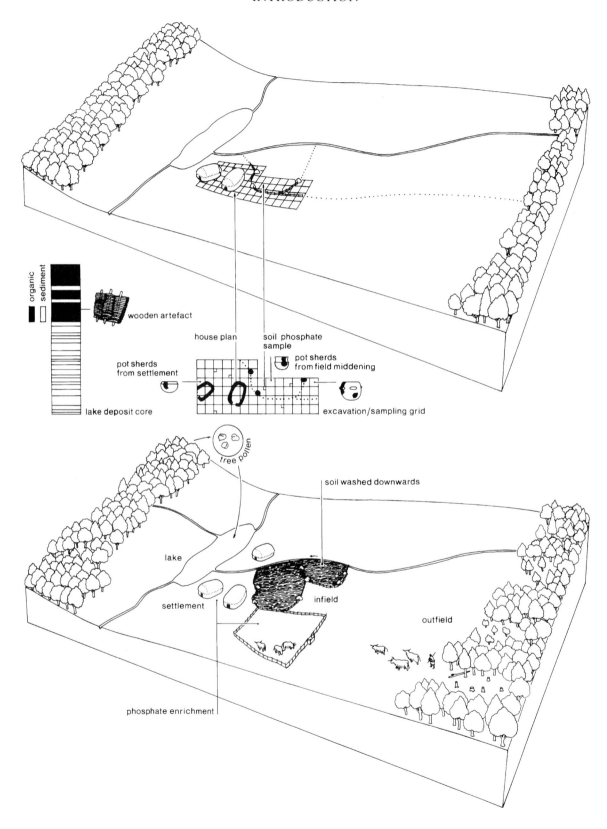

organic sediment

wooden artefact

lake deposit core

house plan

soil phosphate sample

pot sherds from settlement

pot sherds from field middening

excavation/sampling grid

tree pollen

soil washed downwards

lake

settlement

infield

outfield

phosphate enrichment

3 *The lower block diagram shows how an ancient landscape might have looked about 3500. To left middle is a representation of the layers of sediments and organic peat which built up in the lochan. The lower ones were composed partly of soil washed down from ploughed fields, preserving pollen which allows reconstruction of the local vegetation. The upper sedge peats built up as the lochan became shallow, and a stretch of wattle fence thrown into the lochan was preserved in them. An archaeological excavation (shown in the middle) revealed part of the settlement and field systems. The top diagram shows how scientists working together might reconstruct the ancient landscape, getting it basically right despite inadequate data.*

only rarely that the evidence can be interpreted in a simple and unambiguous way (**3**).

Often what those who study ancient environments record is only an indirect measure of what they, and most archaeologists, are really interested in. For instance, the relative widths of the rings of wood built up each year by trees have some relationship to climate. But bad conditions for an individual tree do not necessarily mean bad conditions for a pasture field half a kilometre away. Perhaps the tree suffered from fungus that year, and anyway, an ideal climate for a tree may be less than perfect for a farmer.

Like archaeology, palaeoenvironmental studies were revolutionized when Willard Libby invented radiocarbon dating in the mid-1950s. For the first time, peat and the organic remains often preserved in soils and sediments could be dated and thus changes in vegetation and other information could be matched chronologically with layers and structures on archaeological sites.

Radiocarbon dating

Radiocarbon is a radioactive form of carbon created in the upper atmosphere by cosmic rays. It mixes quite rapidly into the lower atmosphere and the sea, and it is used by plants like ordinary carbon; but, unlike ordinary carbon, it decays. However much radiocarbon a plant has in it at the moment it stops growing, half of the radiocarbon will have disintegrated after 5730 years. Libby's genius, for which he received a Nobel prize, was to realize that this decay could be treated as a sort of clock. An old bit of plant material which had only half the radiocarbon one might expect in a modern plant growing in similar conditions must be about 5730 years old. Because animals eat plants, the carbon in their bodies too contains much the same proportion of radiocarbon to ordinary carbon as in the atmosphere; so animal remains can also be dated (**4**).

However, it was shown in the 1970s, by dating of long sequences of tree rings, that the proportion has varied over both short time-scales and long ones. The long-term variation meant that radiocarbon dates were in general 'too young', by as much as 1000 years for wood from 9000 years ago. The short-term variations were big enough that a single radiocarbon date could correspond to any one of several calendar dates. However, by comparing a radiocarbon measurement with those on tree rings of known age, it can be calibrated to give a true date estimate, usually with a twenty to one chance that it lies within a two to three hundred year span centred on the best estimate (**5**).

With careful selection of several samples (rather than just one), careful physical and chemical separation of the fraction of the sample which is to be dated, and meticulous measurement of all the error sources which influence the raw result, fairly reliable date estimates can be obtained.

Long before the discovery of radiocarbon dating, archaeologists estimated dates on the basis that stone tools preceded bronze tools, which in turn preceded iron tools. This intellectual structure was called the Three Age System, and labels like 'The Neolithic', 'The Bronze Age' and 'The Iron Age' were used to typify long periods of time. As archaeology developed, estimates of the relative dates of

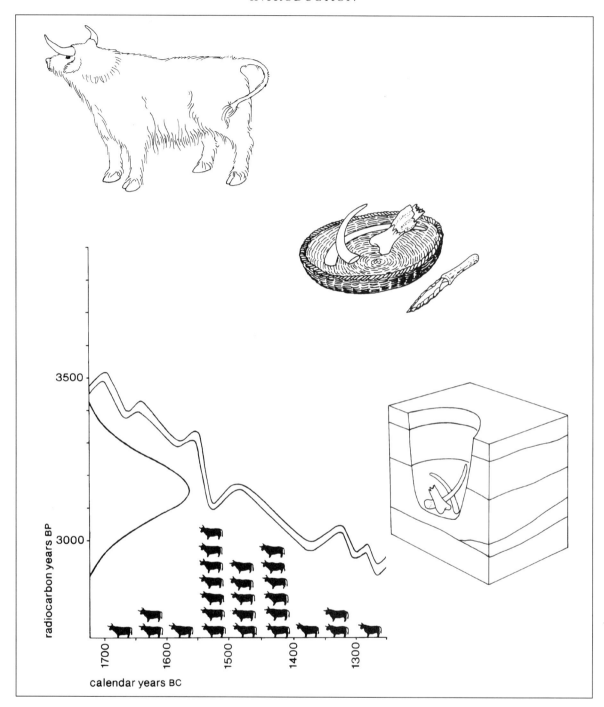

3500

3000

radiocarbon years BP

1700   1600   1500   1400   1300

calendar years BC

4 *The ratio of radiocarbon to ordinary carbon in an animal's bones depends, while it is alive, on that in what it eats, which in turn depends on that in the air. Once the animal dies, the ratio diminishes steadily. The time since it died is estimated by measuring the ratio and comparing it with that in tree rings of known date. The neat curve on the vertical axis of the diagram is an interpretation of the measured ratio of radioactive to normal carbon in the animal bone in 'radiocarbon years'. The columns of cows on the horizontal axis represent the probabilities that the animal died in particular fifty-year periods of real years.*

structures and objects were built up in three ways. Excavations on archaeological sites showed which structures and objects occurred earlier or later than others. Technologically sophisticated tools and weapons were assumed to be later, in general, than cruder ones. Assessments of true age were reached through comparisons with literate societies like those of the Near East.

These methods led to underestimates of the true age of Scottish prehistoric sites. Structures and objects found in Scotland were assumed to be poor imitations of broadly similar objects found in the ancient civilizations. Since Scottish structures and objects would not be direct copies, but rather imitations of north-west European imitations of south-east European imitations of the originals, it was supposed that Scottish structures and objects must be much later than similar ones in the Near East or Egypt.

5 Long sequences of tree rings can be built up by matching those in trees of overlapping date. In the diagram to the right, the ratio of radiocarbon to ordinary carbon in ten- or twenty-year blocks of tree rings is expressed in 'radiocarbon years' and plotted against real years. Short-term variations have been smoothed out in this diagram.

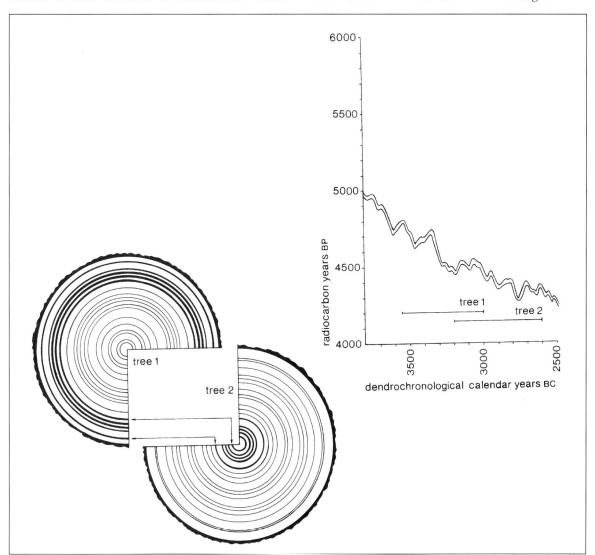

In general, the broad sequence of Scottish prehistory which had been developed by the 1950s was sound, even though the absolute dates attached to the parts of that sequence were wrong. Radiocarbon dating, however, has given us a new way of looking at the diversity of human endeavours in ancient times. With true dates we can identify long periods of little change and short periods of rapid change. Everywhere we look there is evidence of vigour and variety. We can say, for instance, that particular methods of ploughing, and types of structure, tool or weapon, were earlier in one area than another, or, conversely, that they were of much the same date in different areas. We can build on this information to create pictures of past societies which make few initial assumptions about the ways that each influenced the others.

All dates in the text will be calibrated (that is to say, approximately calendar) dates, achieved by reference to radiocarbon-dated tree rings. I have used a set of tables called the 'bidecadal tree ring data set' produced by combining measurements made from several different laboratories and published by M. Stuiver and G. Pearson in the journal *Radiocarbon* in 1993.

In general, I shall describe what happened within 500-year-long periods of time, for instance 3000 to 2500 BC. I shall normally omit the 'BC' in the text. I shall often refer to generations to express periods of several centuries. We do not know how many human generations there were per 500 years in Scotland during prehistory. I shall assume there were 20 (that is, generations of 25 years each) although the average probably varied from place to place and time to time.

Often enough a radiocarbon date which most likely lies close to the beginning of one period is only somewhat more likely to belong to that period than to the period before. Similarly, a date which lies near the end of a period is only somewhat more likely to belong to that period than to the following one. Where the date of a house, tomb or other structure is more or less equally likely to belong to one of two periods, I have often put it in the later period, since what is found in a pit or post-hole ceased to live, and thus ceased to take up fresh radiocarbon, before (sometimes long before) the time it got caught up in the pit or post-hole.

The art of the conjurer

I have had to make some hard choices about what to leave out. I shall mention only a few sites which are not dated by radiocarbon and I shall mention very few Irish, English, Welsh or continental sites. It should be obvious that modern national boundaries are artificial, and that the sea connected people as much as or more than it separated them. Nevertheless, many previous attempts to describe what happened in Scotland during the period covered in this book have been strongly coloured by interpretations of what has been found in neighbouring countries, while here I am concerned to build up a picture based so far as possible entirely on radiocarbon-dated Scottish sites and artefacts; for there is a great need for regional studies which can form the basis for subsequent geographically broader comparisons. Nevertheless, most of the ideas presented in this book are the result of generations of hard work, based on wide comparisons, before radiocarbon dating was invented. The study of this spider's web of evidence, this building up of patterns from threads is still the art, as John Aubrey put it more than three hundred years ago, of 'a Conjurer, who makes those walke and appeare that have layen in their graves many hundreds of yeares : and to represent as it were to the eie, the places, Customes and Fashions, that were of old Times'.

CHAPTER ONE

An Untilled Land

Hunters and gatherers

Proof that there were people in Scotland for thousands of years before the first farmers depended for a long time on stray finds of their characteristic stone tools, on deposits of food debris and antler and bone tools in a few caves around Oban and on mounds of sea shells on the islands of the Inner Hebrides and along the Forth valley. Flint and other small stone tools were (and still are) turned up by agricultural ploughing in the river valleys of southern and eastern Scotland, by forestry ploughing in the uplands and by natural erosion in sand-dune areas. None of these finds was properly dated before the invention of radiocarbon dating, and many of the collections included much later flints. In addition there were a few stray finds of antler hunting tools, like those discovered with whale skeletons beneath the clay which filled in the ancient upper estuary of the Forth.

Scotland was covered by ice during the last glaciation. Around 13,500 there was rapid warming to temperatures quite like those of today, followed by a long cold snap between about 11,000 and 10,000. Gradually juniper and other shrubs covered the tundra. Around 9000, birches began to form forests in southern Scotland, followed about 8250 by hazel; both species spread north rapidly. By 8000, birch had reached the far north of Scotland. About 7500, elms began to appear in southern Scotland. By now average temperatures had risen until they

were higher than those of today, while rainfall was about 90 per cent of present levels.

Oak trees started to grow in southern Scotland about 6700, and over the next five hundred years they followed the spread of elm into central Scotland and then along the east coast to the area round Inverness and along the west coast throughout mainland Argyll. No doubt Scots pine had spread earlier, for it colonized the Grampians between 6300 and 5500, creating the Caledonian Forest.

The earliest known settlement is at Kinloch, on the island of Rum. The people who settled at Kinloch about 7500 found the island mostly covered by open heathland and shrubs like juniper, but with birch and hazel growing in the more sheltered areas. They settled by a stream which ran down to salt-marshes; the sea was locally slightly further from the present shore than it is now. Their houses and their boats were probably made of light poles and rods covered by animal skins. They made a variety of tools from flinty beach pebbles and from a stone peculiar to the island, Rum bloodstone. The tools included arrowheads, scrapers and awls, from which we can deduce that these people hunted and worked leather and wood. The people probably used Kinloch as a base camp all year round, hunting on the island and fishing the surrounding waters. They collected hazelnuts and roasted them on their fires. The soils of the settlement were not very suitable for the preservation of bone, so we do not know exactly what animals and birds they hunted, what fish they caught nor what shellfish they collected. But all the signs are that they would have had a rich and varied diet.

Given the rich natural resources of the area, it is hardly surprising that people used this base camp, off and on, for around one thousand years, at least until 6500. That they had abundant contacts with other people in the area seems very likely, for Rum bloodstone, a particular stone they used in addition to flint, has been found on other sites within a 50km (30 miles) radius of Rum.

Kinloch is very important to our understanding of the early peoples of Scotland. It shows (although at the same time that Kinloch was dug, other work was starting which would independently prove the same point) that hunters and gatherers settled here long before elm and oak had spread into western Scotland. It helps make the people who lived in Scotland at this time seem like those of the rest of Europe.

Another early settlement, at Morton in Fife, has long been important to ideas about the way of life of the hunter-gatherers. For part of the period between 7000 and 5000 Morton was an island, for a sea-level rise caused by still melting ice had outpaced the gentle rise of Scotland which followed removal of the great weight of ice-sheets and glaciers. There are technical difficulties with the earlier radiocarbon dates from the site, and I shall not discuss it further, except to say that for a long time it reinforced a belief that the main camps of the hunter-gatherers were concentrated on the coast, although it was accepted that they may have exploited inland areas. Recent excavations at Biggar Common in Upper Clydesdale have revealed a dozen stake- and post-holes preserved under a much later burial mound, forming what seems to be part of a small sub-rectangular timber structure dating to within a few centuries either way of 5000. Although only one flint of a type characteristic of the hunter-gatherers was found under the mound, there is very abundant evidence that they made flint tools elsewhere on Biggar Common. With the increasing amount of evi-

dence of disturbance of the forest by burning, there is now every reason to suppose that there were base camps in many inland areas even if the coastal areas were in general more attractive.

Farmers in the lands facing Scotland

Very broadly, there were two early groups of farmers in north-west Europe. On the light soils of Germany and lands further south and east many large settlements have been found. They consisted of groups of substantial timber longhouses. The settlements are broadly linked together by the house type and by the pottery, which is, characteristically, round bottomed with incised bands of decoration. Well before 5000 there were settlements of this kind in western Germany and the Netherlands. On the other hand, in south-western France, and along the north shore of the Mediterranean, there were settlements of farmers living in rectangular houses with pottery decorated by pressing the edges of cockle shells into the wet clay. In north-west France people continued with a hunting and gathering way of life even after 5000. Meanwhile, on the coasts of Denmark, people who lived by fishing, gathering shellfish and plants, and hunting had adopted pottery and domesticated pigs. These Danish groups show no signs that they had taken up agriculture. It is thought that they were able to settle in the same place all year round because of rich fishing grounds.

Over the next five hundred years farming became a common way of life in northern France and the Netherlands. The Danish coastal groups took up agriculture too. Around 4500, then, farming, supplemented by hunting, fishing and gathering, was the predominant way of life in all the lands facing Britain.

Scotland at the dawn of farming

Between 4500 and 4000 Scotland was not completely blanketed by forest (**6**). There were clearings and good grazing on the edges of the

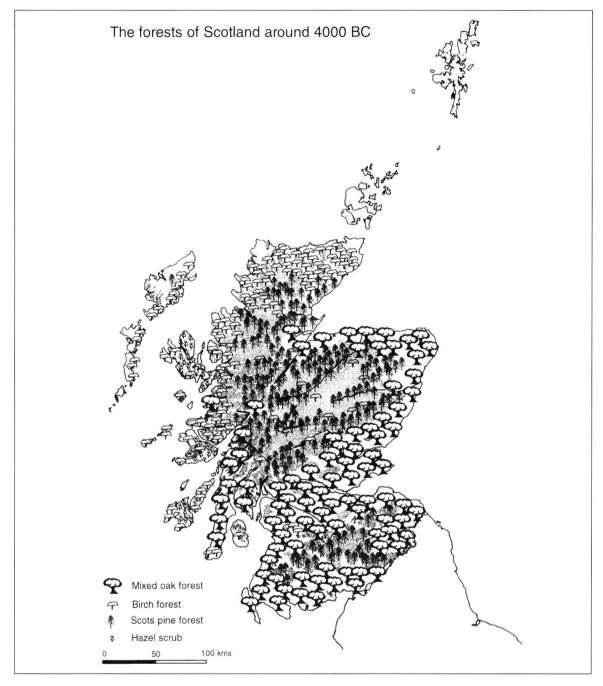

The forests of Scotland around 4000 BC

Mixed oak forest
Birch forest
Scots pine forest
Hazel scrub
0   50   100 kms

6 *The forests of Scotland about 4000, before farming had made a major impact on them (after Bennett, 1989).*

uplands and in the lowlands around lakes, river courses and marshy areas. In the forests, the woodland trees had been improving the soils for two or three thousand years. Their

roots had reached down, bringing up nutrients, and rotting leaves added organic matter to the harsh post-glacial soils. Brown earths, as these fertile forest soils are called, had developed below the higher hilltops in much of Scotland.

A century or so before this date we can see fairly clear evidence of management of the woodlands of the Borders. Parts of the upper margins of the woods, much higher, at around 350–400m (1200–1300ft), than they naturally are today, were burnt. So, it seems, were the lowland margins of some lakes and fens. The traditional explanation for this is that hunters were firing woodland to improve pasture for red deer and encourage them to concentrate at known spots. Before looking at other possibilities, let us consider how large the hunting populations were around 4500, and what that implies about their way of life.

More recent peoples of deciduous forests in other parts of the world, with a similar level of technology, are recorded as having an average population density of about 10–20 people for every 1000sq km (400sq miles). So if each group of Scottish hunter-gatherers consisted of, say, 10–20 people, between one and four such groups would have controlled the coastal plains and the northern sides of the Lammermuirs, Moorfoots and the Pentlands from Berwick-upon-Tweed to Edinburgh. At first sight this may seem a ridiculously low estimate. However, what controls the long-term population of an area is not how well the people can live in good times, but how well they cope with bad times. That said, the sea and rivers would have provided fish and shellfish. The uplands would have allowed hunting. In the forests were more deer, and wild cattle. The fruits and roots of wild plants could be collected, and hazelnuts could be stored against lean times. Beach pebbles of flint and chert (a flint-like quartz) could be used to create tools, and, as we have seen, other sources of stone, such as Rum bloodstone, were exploited. Perhaps most important of all for long-term survival, the hunter-gatherers had productive contacts with neighbouring groups. They interbred, and in hard times the kinship links between groups would have helped them to support each other against adversity. Since human groups which are successful over the long term seem to require breeding populations of a few hundred, people must have travelled long distances to

7 *The things which characterize the new farmers for archaeologists – the things which can be dated to around 4000 and later – are large burial mounds (long barrows made of earth and timber, or stone-built burial chambers covered by cairns); houses built of stone, timber or turf; rectilinear timber structures, round-bottomed pottery, leaf-shaped arrowheads, polished stone axeheads, grain, domestic animals, and the habit of digging pits and burying broken pots (and other things) in them. Pollen diagrams demonstrate (rather than merely suggest) the growing of cereals. Increasingly, fragments of fields are being recognized, surviving sealed beneath burial mounds or drifts of shell-sand, although none is yet radiocarbon dated before about 3000. Of all these characteristic things, only polished stone axes can be shown to have been used by the early hunter-gatherers, and that, so far, in Ireland rather than Scotland.*

find suitable marriage partners. In some recorded hunter-gatherer societies it was the young women who married out of the family; in others it was the young men. Either way, we can envisage that there were long-distance kinship connections between groups, and the mobility that this implies goes a long way to explaining why the material culture of the Scottish hunter-gatherers is not very variable: they would have exchanged ideas, food and raw materials on a regular basis. Exchange may have taken the form of barter or of gift exchange; which is to say that gifts may have been given and not returned in kind until later, for that would have simplified exchange of seasonal produce for goods available at a different time of the year, or allowed debts to be stored up against lean times.

The interaction of the hunters with the first farmers was probably complex, but there is some evidence that 4000 (give or take two centuries) is the sensible date to bear in mind when trying to distinguish between predominantly hunting and predominantly farming populations. Nearly all the 23 Scottish radiocarbon dates for archaeological sites centring in the period 4500–4000 are from hunter-gatherer sites or from ones without clear

cultural ties, while most of the 27 dates from 4000–3750 are from sites built by farmers (7).

However, modern theories about complex systems suggest that most such large-scale changes start sporadically, particularly when they involve groups of people well established in different patterns of living. Swift and wide-spread change may turn out to be a special case in a wider theory of change. Farmers probably crossed over the Channel and the North Sea to

Ireland and Britain at many times between about 5000 and 4000, or at least between 4500 and 4000. Quite probably they did so in family groups, and it may be that many of the early groups turned to less intensive farming methods than they had been accustomed to; for economic systems characterized by permanent settlements and draught animals are not necessarily stable when people move into fertile areas with a low indigenous population.

The seemingly most attractive kinds of agriculture known today, if unclaimed land is plentiful, are non-intensive. Pioneer farmers burn small patches of virgin forest, and roots or cereals are planted direct into the ashes. After the farmers have moved to another plot of land, secondary forest grows in the clearing and the farmers may not return to that spot for a generation or more; but return they do, for it is easier to turn the young forest to a new field than it is to convert primary forest. This farming system involves a territory in which, in any given year, about 5 per cent of the area is under crops, 40–50 per cent can loosely be described as bush or scrub (young trees, bushes, herbs and grasses including, in Scotland, fairly abundant hazel) and 45–55 per cent is secondary forest consisting largely of trees aged no more than 20–25 years. Round the edges of the farming area the virgin forest remains, if the territory does not link up directly with that controlled by another group.

This type of farming requires no large domestic animals; hoes or digging-sticks are used, rather than spades or ploughs. Indeed the tree and bush roots in the newly cleared areas make ploughing difficult. The people do not need to weed fields, because the land is abandoned after one or two crops have been grown on it and weeds do not have time to establish themselves. Such systems allow plenty of time for more pleasurable pursuits than weeding or caring for cows and sheep or goats: the varied habitats provided by the different ages of bush and forest provide rich hunting and many wild roots, seeds and fruits.

Thus, since farming in the secondary forest provides more leisure than maintaining farmland, and more than clearing new areas of primary forest, it seems quite likely that some family groups – perhaps many – would adopt this way of life even if they had come from an area in which more intensive farming systems were common. Ester Boserup noted in her book, *The Conditions of Agricultural Growth* (1965), that 'cultivators who use intensive methods in their densely settled home districts give up these methods after they have been resettled in less densely populated districts and given more land per family. Many settlement areas, meant to serve as model farms for the local population, provide sad sights of poor yields obtained from unweeded and unwatered fields.' Boserup's conclusions were based largely on tropical and sub-tropical farming systems, and it is always dangerous to use accounts of what happened in distant parts of the world to explain what happened close to home; but it is perfectly proper to allow such anecdotes to widen the range of possibilities we should consider. Application of Boserup's ideas to north-west Europe was criticized in the 1980s because the evidence traditionally supposed to demonstrate non-intensive agricultural systems there was inadequate; but it is not obvious how we would distinguish the traces left by such a system from those that would be produced by hunters burning patches of forest. Pollen diagrams would continue to show an abundance of trees, and this easy life need not have left many traces of structures since woodland would have re-invaded cleared areas including those in which houses had been built.

Some prehistorians suggest a different interpretation of the change from hunting to farming. Agriculture may have developed within fairly static hunting and gathering populations. The really important difference may be that between settled people and wanderers. On the coasts of Denmark hunter-gatherers who had lived a fairly settled existence dependent on rich inshore fishing developed pottery and bred domesticated pigs around 5000–4750. Their way of life survived for one thousand years before they turned to agriculture. Perhaps the hunter-gatherers of Scotland too started to settle well before 4000, living partly on the fish which ran rich in the rivers and inshore waters and partly on semi-domesticated deer and perhaps cattle. Perhaps they gradually started to plant wheat and barley in clearings in the forest, the seed obtained initially from people living further to the south and east. To complicate the possibilities still further, there is evidence from America and Australia that hunting groups built generally long and low lines of stones or slight banks where the scattered hunter-gatherer families met to reinforce their social ties. It may be that some Scottish monuments discovered during the past decade will prove to have been built well before people began to practise agriculture. And it may even be that the invention of chambered tombs, which are found mainly in those areas of northern and western Europe where hunters would have controlled the land longest, arose from a mixture of indigenous and imported traditions.

Until early hunter-gatherer burials are discovered and the biochemistry of their bones compared with that of the bones of farmers there will be no way of telling whether the tombs and houses built after 4000 were constructed by descendants of the hunters or by incoming agriculturists. That said, it is probably more likely that incoming farmers took up a less arduous way of life than that hunters took up a more arduous one.

By 4000 there was a definite change from the circumstances of half a millennium earlier. The people who still relied on hunting, fishing and gathering had had to change the way they looked at the world. Theirs was no longer the only way to survive. Perhaps it had become a very risky way of living as the areas claimed by non-intensive farmers – some of them perhaps their own folk – increased. The hunters were perhaps still more knowledgeable than the farmers about sources of raw materials such as

flint and stone suitable for making stone axes. They could probably find game when the farmers could not, even if the animals they hunted had been forced to adapt to the presence of areas cleared for farming and a greater proportion of secondary forest. As we shall see when discussing the particularly Scottish expression of this change, the farmers probably also lived in small groups and no doubt they and the hunting people sometimes interbred. No doubt also they sometimes succoured each other in time of need; and at other times and in other places, perhaps because of contempt for a different way of life, they fought each other, each defending traditional resources and their own way of life.

It was also around 4000 that the next stage of intensification of farming started in some parts of Scotland. Areas cleared of forest by fire had not usually been ploughed, because of the work required to grub up the roots of bushes and trees, but now secondary forest was replaced locally by grasslands as the areas under more intensive cultivation near settlements increased. The old method of clearing land by fire did not kill off grasses because their roots survived. It was difficult to hoe or use red deer antlers or digging-sticks to break up grasslands. Ploughs pulled by people or draught cattle were the only way to secure food for a growing population, if there was not much unclaimed forest. Yet farmers who used draught animals to plough their fields had a more arduous way of life. They had to care for their animals as well as grow their crops, and thus they must either have maintained natural fodder over an area considerably larger than that under cultivation, or grown fodder. The beast pulling a primitive ard (a simple form of plough used to break up the turf before cultivation by spade or hoe) could plough only a hectare or so in the ploughing season, and perhaps 50 per cent of the ploughed area had to be used for feeding the draught animals if pasture was not available. Probably, though, the populations in some areas had grown sufficiently that ploughing, and thus the use of draught animals, had become a necessity. It may have been as early as this that individual ownership of land by a family arose, but what little evidence we have from 4000 to 3500 suggests that this was not so.

Whether the indigenous hunter-gatherers of Scotland played a large or small part in the introduction of agriculture (and as I have explained above I think it was small), what does seem to be agreed among most of those studying the prehistory of Britain and Ireland between 4500 and 3500 is that ideas about large-scale invasions, or equally romantic ideas about hunters taking up farming solely because they had had slight contact with distant farmers, are vastly over-simplified. But let us turn from these generalizations to look in more detail at what happened in Scotland.

CHAPTER TWO

Farmers from 4000 to 3500 BC

Ploughs and tombs

People needed a diverse stock of ways to keep themselves fed, and of rituals to ensure reasonable social stability, as their circumstances changed. Throughout prehistory, this set of possible responses was kept rich and diverse in three ways: through oral tradition, through observation of other groups nearby who were using a different set of techniques, and (perhaps somewhat later than this period) physical evidence in the form of old field systems and other structures. Around 4000, more and more groups of people began to favour some of the more arduous responses from the repertoire available to them, most likely because cropping rights in the local fertile areas were already claimed, or because hunting groups made settlement in new areas hazardous. Alongside non-intensive farming in areas of secondary forest, there were areas of pasture and areas in which the land was ploughed with only short periods of fallow. Elsewhere the virgin forest remained.

Houses or special places for disposal of the dead have been found in many of the regions of mainland Scotland. In addition there are ceremonial structures and intriguing hints of rituals bound in with everyday life. Over this 500-year period regional variations grew stronger, leading most notably to differences between the special places which were created for disposal of the dead. The most characteristic surviving burial structures of this period are the chambered tombs of the west and north of Scotland, even though other kinds of sites were preferred for deposition of bodies in the eastern and southern lowlands.

Chambered tombs were mounds of earth, turf or stone containing burial chambers, usually built of stone. The mounds could be roughly square, round, or shaped like the bottom of a shoe-heel, or long compared to their width. Some had horns projecting to either side of the entrance to the chamber. At some tombs a distinct passage connected the outside world to the chamber, and at others the chamber opened straight out of the mound. The burial chamber was sometimes small and simple, but often it was divided into compartments by slabs set into the chamber walls or floor; other tombs contained a main chamber and side or end cells. Many of the chambers were corbelled; that is to say, as the walls were built up, each stone projected a little further inward. Thus the width of the chamber diminished with height until it could be roofed over with slabs. The corbelled walls were prevented from collapsing by an external cairn, which pressed down on the back ends of the wall-stones.

Chambered tombs can be thought of as houses of the dead. The great majority of people, in all those preliterate settled societies which have been studied by anthropologists, believe in an afterlife. The dead retain the social position that they held in life, and they

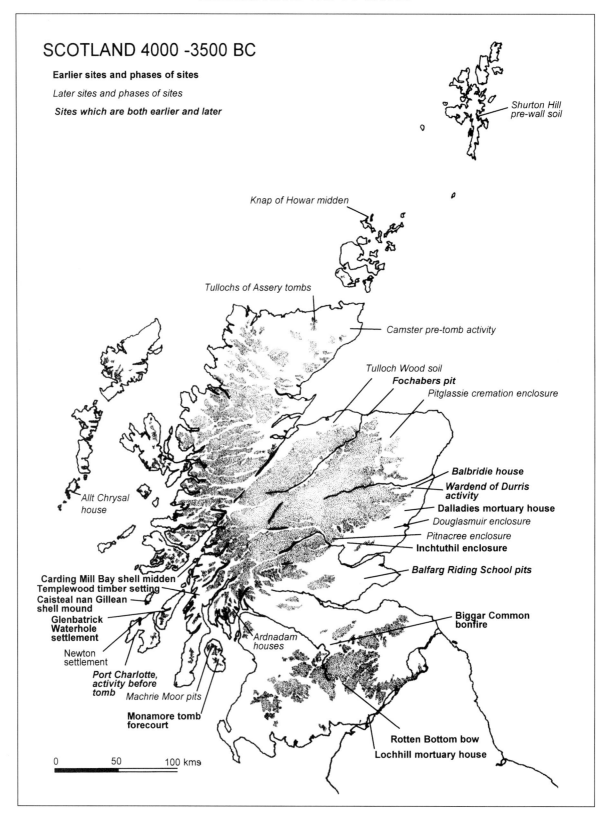

SCOTLAND 4000 -3500 BC

Earlier sites and phases of sites

Later sites and phases of sites

Sites which are both earlier and later

Shurton Hill
pre-wall soil

Knap of Howar midden

Tullochs of Assery tombs

Camster pre-tomb activity

Tulloch Wood soil
Fochabers pit
Pitglassie cremation enclosure

Balbridie house
***Wardend of Durris
activity***
Dalladies mortuary house
Douglasmuir enclosure
Pitnacree enclosure
Inchtuthil enclosure

Balfarg Riding School pits

Allt Chrysal
house

Carding Mill Bay shell midden
Templewood timber setting
**Caisteal nan Gillean
shell mound**
**Glenbatrick
Waterhole
settlement**
Newton
settlement
***Port Charlotte,
activity before
tomb***
Machrie Moor pits

**Monamore tomb
forecourt**

*Ardnadam
houses*

**Biggar Common
bonfire**

Rotten Bottom bow
Lochhill mortuary house

0   50   100 kms

need help in their journey to join their dead kinsfolk. Burial ceremonies and grave-goods ensure they will be received properly into their next existence. The spirits of the dead are powerful and can appear among mortals; and they are not always friendly.

Commonly, the soul is thought to consist of two or more spiritual entities. There is a body soul (or breath soul) which leaves the body with its last breath, and returns to some universal stock of life-force. Then there is a dream soul (or free soul), often thought of as remaining in the dead body until it has been completely changed by decomposition, or cremation, or some other process. Sometimes there are other spirits, such as an ego soul which retains a sense of personal identity. Beliefs of this kind are so universally held by recorded preliterate settled societies that it seems likely that the tomb-builders shared some variant of them.

Accounts of chambered tombs and their contents are like descriptions of masks. Masks are symbols of ideas, and so in a sense are the remains of tombs; and behind them was a complex, living reality. It is not, at present, possible to prove that any particular combination of tomb architecture, bones and grave-goods represented one particular set of beliefs. However, the descriptions that follow should be read with an awareness that the tomb-builders probably thought either that parts of the souls of the dead celebrated or endured the afterlife in the tombs until their bodies disintegrated, or that the tombs provided a resting place until the free spirits were ready to set out on a journey to join their kin in some other place, or that by placing bodies in the tombs they could stop their spirits from causing harm to the living.

I shall describe the sites dated to this period in a great loop from north to south along the east coast, and then northward again to the Western Isles (8).

8 *Map of sites radiocarbon dated to between 4000 and 3500.*

The north

There is no direct evidence for settlement in Orkney or Shetland in this period. Around 4000, Caithness was a land of birch forests and mires. Even though it was, on average, warmer than today by a degree or two, it will have been windswept. There is no direct evidence for settlement in Caithness during the first half of this period, but chambered tombs were constructed between 3750 and 3500.

Three chambered cairns cluster round the outflow from Loch Calder, 10km (6 miles) inland from Dounreay: Tulloch of Assery A and B, and Tulach an t'Sionnaich (9). Carefully built from fine Caithness slabs, Tulloch of Assery A had a ground-plan like an ox-skin: a body reaching north and south with legs stretching out diagonally from the corners. At either end of the cairn short passages led into irregular chambers, divided by vertical side slabs into three compartments and roofed over by long stones. In the northern chamber were two low benches bearing disarticulated human bones, and on top of collapsed building slabs in the centre of the chamber was a much later crouched burial dating after 1500.

Tulloch of Assery B, in complete contrast, was a round cairn with a passage and a rectangular chamber divided very neatly into three compartments. The dates in this period were from charcoal on the old ground surface under the cairn and from animal bone found on the chamber floor. Use of the chamber went on until after 3000, and the tomb was sealed up after 2500. When excavated, the chamber contained fragmentary remains of several human skeletons. One of them, piled with another in the centre of the chamber, was of an elderly man who had been shot in the lower back, for a flint arrowhead was found in his spine.

Tulach an t'Sionnaich is today a long low cairn; at its southern end it rises to nearly 2m (6ft) in height. Excavation showed a complex construction sequence. Earliest of all were traces of a rough wall of unknown purpose.

9 *The three chambered tombs at the north end of Loch Calder in Caithness, northern Scotland, are called (from left to right) Tulloch of Assery B, Tulloch of Assery A, and Tulach an t'Sionnaich. Their burial chambers differ in size and shape. Similar small groups of tombs are abundant in northern and western Scotland.*

Then a small round cairn was built, surrounding and helping to stabilize an almost square burial chamber entered from the south end of the cairn by a short passage. Human bones found on the chamber floor were brought into the tomb between 3500 and 3250. The round cairn was then encased in a heel-shaped cairn, the façade of which completely blocked the entrance passage. The heel-shaped cairn was subsequently enlarged and the long tail of the cairn was added, making the cairn 58m (190ft) long. The chamber was purposefully filled up after 2500. Finally, a cremation in an urn was buried in the collapsed front of the cairn, probably centuries later again.

The long cairn at Camster, Caithness, tells a variant of this story. The dates all belong in the ten generations before 3500, and come from informal hearths amid a scatter of post-holes, small flints of hunter-gatherer type, and round-bottomed pottery. Subsequently (perhaps generations later) two small round cairns were built, one with a small simple chamber like that in Tulach an t'Sionnaich and the other more like those under the Tullochs of Assery. The cairns were designed to hold down the back ends of the slabs forming the chamber walls rather than to be burial monuments in their own right; and the building of the long cairn started shortly after that of the round cairns. The long cairn had neat side-walls, but the stones inside these walls were just dumped in, and rough transverse lines of stones suggest the beginning and ending of short phases of building, perhaps over several years. At either end, curving forecourts were outlined by hornworks.

Curiously, although the chamber and tomb shapes at Loch Calder and Camster represent fairly well the variations found in Caithness, the chamber contents are not typical. Excavations in the nineteenth century showed that many burial chambers in Caithness contained thick black layers with both heavily and partially burnt human bones. Both above and below these layers were unburnt human bones; the skeletons on top seem to have been fairly complete. Fires were lit in the chambers, scorching the stones. The overall impression is that incomplete skeletons and domestic rubbish, earth and stones were brought into the chamber and that the human bones were smashed up and burnt. It is impossible to know what went on in the minds of those engaged in these rituals, but it seems that they thought people needed the same things in an afterlife as they needed when alive. However, there is an impression of use of the tombs over great lengths of time, and perhaps archaeologists vastly underestimate changes in ritual practices over those periods.

The fertile lands at the head of the Moray Firth were rich in oak and elm woodland around 4000. The area had been exploited by hunter-gatherers over the previous two thousand years, and probably as in so much of Scotland the area was a mosaic of open land, secondary woodland and forests. People were active at Raigmore near Inverness between 4000 and 3750. They buried charcoal in a pit with cremated bone, and, in another pit, a stone slab bearing a single cup-mark. Taking this at face value (although it is always possible that the charcoal was old at the time it was put into the pit, having lain around on the site for centuries, and there are technical difficulties with the dates from Raigmore) this gives us the earliest date for rock-carving in Britain.

The north-east

Around 4000 the coastal parts of north-east Scotland were dominated by oak and elm, and the margins of the Grampians by Scots pine. There are plentiful signs that the natural vegetation was disturbed between 4000 and 3750, but none of the earthen long barrows north of the Mounth, some of which may date to this period, have been excavated.

In the next ten generations, leading up to 3500, there is evidence of burials, settlements and more obscure activities. Near Fochabers, under a sandy mound, there was a layer of charcoal containing abundant Neolithic pottery,

10 *At Midtown of Pitglassie, in north-eastern Scotland, a roughly circular area about 12m (40ft) across was used for deposition of cremated human bodies. The photograph shows the site during excavation. Two of about twelve settings for a ring of upright stones are visible as dark splodges, at top centre and top right.*

and a pit. Perhaps the site was, at this period, a settlement or a hunting camp; but if the equation of a settled way of life with pottery is correct, the hunters probably came from a farming community.

From Pitglassie comes evidence for a markedly different type of burial ritual from those dated in Caithness to the ten-generation period before 3500. Its only similarity is that it involved the deposition of bones in a special place. Turf and stones were cleared from a roughly circular area and a funeral pyre was lit

on it; the next activity was burial of cremations in the area. At some stage during these rituals 11–12 post settings defined the roughly circular area. Then turf and stone (perhaps that cleared from the site at the beginning) was piled up to form a ring cairn. At some later date – perhaps much later – the interior was covered by a cairn and then, later again, a burial cist was inserted. The cremation area at Pitglassie is important because it has some similarities to the later ritual and burial monuments in north-east Scotland, which are quite unlike those of much of the rest of Scotland (**10**).

Within the same 250-year period a great timber hall was built at Balbridie, on Deeside. Although it is difficult to find identical buildings elsewhere, similar ones are found in north-west France. Others in the Netherlands are not very different. The plant remains from Balbridie were described by the excavators as a processed crop of European type. It seems there was some sort of direct connection between Scotland and the continent, at least in the two or three centuries before 3500 (**11**).

11 *Balbridie timber hall, in north-eastern Scotland, measured 26 by 13m (85 by 43ft). This model, part of a display at the British Museum, shows to the left the structure of the house and to the right how it may have looked when it was in use.*

The hall was big enough to hold thirty to fifty people. Situated on the banks of the Dee, it was on a natural route into the heart of north-east Scotland. The Dee was a good salmon river, and its well-drained terraces of light gravels and alluvium were ideal for agriculture. Woodlands were close to hand and pasture-covered hills not far away to the south. It was a place of plentiful seasonal resources. The finds from it included round-bottomed bowls, and abundant remains of emmer wheat and bere barley. One or two oat seeds were also found, probably weeds growing in the cereal crops, and fragments of crab-apple. There was also a small cake of flax seed of a domesticated type, suggesting that flax was grown for oil.

The east

Just north of the junction between the Tay and Isla rivers in Perthshire is a quite extraordinary monument, the Cleaven Dyke (**12**). It was probably built in the centuries around 4000. Before the recent excavations which produced radiocarbon dates, other investigations had suggested that the monument was built in woodland following agriculture. Descriptions

12 *The Cleaven Dyke, in eastern Scotland, is 2km (well over 1 mile) long. Where it has not been ploughed, it consists of a 12–20m (40–66ft) wide central bank on flat ground between widely spaced ditches. It was built in segments. Its eastern end, shown here, is now visible only as a cropmark.*

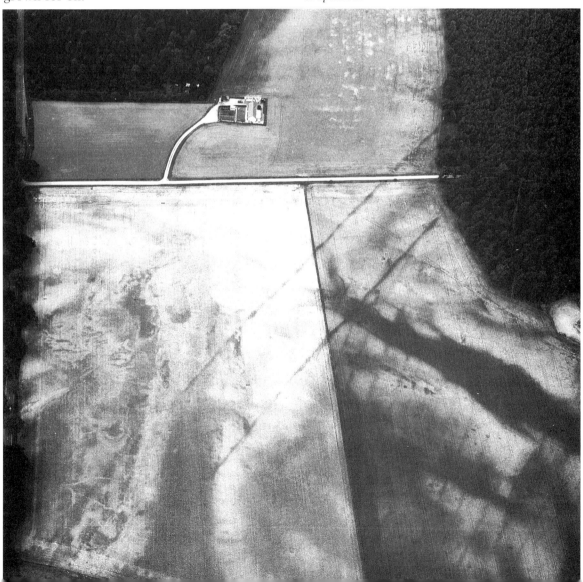

of the soil and buried turf in and under the monument make fascinating reading: 'this was not an area of undisturbed deciduous woodland when the Dyke was constructed, but it had passed through one or more phases of clearance amounting to at least some hundreds of years ... the presence of oak charcoal in the revetting turf is also consistent with human interference with the natural woodland' (*Glasgow Archaeological Journal* 13, 63–9). Although this evidence could be taken to mean the woods had been burnt by hunter-gatherers, it does fit uncannily well with the suggestion that small-scale farming had taken place for many generations before 4000. Indeed, the monument makes much visual sense if we think of it as striking for 2km (over 1 mile) through secondary woodland, strongly outlined by the forest edge. That said, we do not know what function it served. There is a suspicion among archaeologists that its bank is in some way related to earthen long barrows (which in addition to covering burials seem designed to act as foci for local communities) and that its ditches create an internal space related to enclosures revealed by air photography, such as that at Inchtuthil, 3–4km (2–2½ miles) west of the Cleaven Dyke.

The large (except by comparison with the Cleaven Dyke) rectangular timber enclosure at Inchtuthil dates to the first ten generations after 4000. It was built of oak posts and radially split oak planks, some from a tree at least one hundred and ninety years old and remained in use long enough for the fence to require replacement before it was destroyed by fire. It is fashionable to suppose that such enclosures were built for ceremonial dances or displays, or for exposure of the bodies of dead people. Indeed, the Inchtuthil enclosure's combination of length (50m) and width (12m) (165 by 40ft) seems to make a more prosaic use such as a cattle corral unlikely.

A complex rectilinear timber enclosure at Douglasmuir near Friockheim was built a century or two before 3500 (**13**). Defined by

13 *The enclosure at Douglasmuir, in eastern Scotland, shown here during excavation, measured about 65 by 20m (214 by 66ft) overall and was built of stout posts. Presumably they supported a solid fence of wattle or horizontal timbers. The timbers used for the end walls and the central dividing line were sturdier than those used for the sides of the enclosure. There were many pits in the area. One of them, containing pottery, was found inside the enclosure.*

sturdy posts set close to each other, it was divided into two roughly equal halves by another line of posts. It was in an area liberally spattered with pits, and one of these inside the enclosure contained round-bottomed pottery, typical of that used by the farmers of this period, and charcoal which produced a radiocarbon date indistinguishable from those from the post-holes. The likeliest explanations are that it served some function connected with displays or ritual dances, or with exposure of the bodies of the dead. Because the pit-speckled area near the enclosure could not be excavated, we do not know whether there was a settlement near the enclosure or whether (as seems to be the case at other sites) the pits were dug for ritual purposes involving the burial of broken pottery.

A mortuary house (a small but sturdy structure designed to hold remains of the dead) was built at Pitnacree in Strathtay, the valley running up from Dunkeld to Loch Tay, probably at some time between 3800 and 3300 (**14**). The date was taken from a mass of charcoal

lying on an old ground surface, into which had been set two large D-shaped post-holes. With the charcoal was plain round-bottomed pottery. The posts, made from split tree trunks, were over a metre across and set a metre into the ground, and the post-holes each had ramps cut into the ground on one side, of the kind required when levering long, massive timbers into an upright position. The posts will have stood 3–4m (10–13ft) tall.

After use of this structure ceased, a turf and stone structure replaced it. The excavators interpreted it as a horseshoe-shaped mass of

14 *The first building at Pitnacree, in eastern Scotland, was based on two massive split tree trunks set in the ground nearly 3m (9ft) apart. Judging by a better preserved example in northern England, they may have supported a wicker box. This building was replaced by what may either have been a timber and turf chambered tomb or an enclosure. The reconstruction drawing on the left shows it being built as a chamber, about 6 by 2m (20 by 6ft). It may have been entered through a stone passage just over 1m (3½ft) wide and 1.5m (5ft) high. The alternative reconstruction, to the right, assumes a steeply sided turf and stone bank round an open space, which may have been filled in quite swiftly to create a mound.*

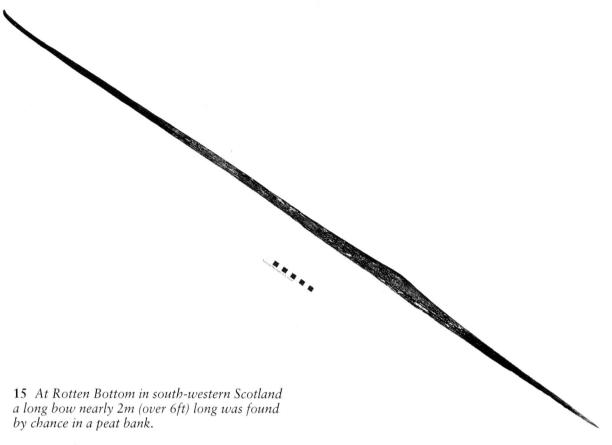

15 *At Rotten Bottom in south-western Scotland a long bow nearly 2m (over 6ft) long was found by chance in a peat bank.*

stones enclosing a narrow open space, reached at the eastern end by a stone-walled and roofed passage, which was later built up to form a mound. Inside it were several cremations. However, the published photographs, plans and sections suggest that it was instead a chambered tomb, with a mound built of stone and turf round a burial chamber probably floored with stones and lined and roofed with timber and turf. If so, the chamber was similar in shape and size to many of the chambers and passages in the cairns of Orkney. Be this as it may, it was a place for disposal of the dead, and cremation was among the burial rites used there. There are about twenty similar mounds in Strathtay. If they were all built for the same purpose they suggest farming flourished there during the fourth millennium.

At Balfarg Riding School in Fife parts of fine, plain, round-bottomed pottery bowls were placed in a pit at some time in the ten generations before 3500. It is particularly worth mentioning because a great ritual centre was later to be built there, and because there seems to be a recurrent pattern of early pits containing pottery on other sites which were to become important centres of activity a thousand or so years later.

The south

There is no dated evidence at all for settlements or burials in Lothian or the Borders between 4000 and 3500; indeed, even the shell middens of the Forth valley show no signs of human activity. A few long barrows are known and they may date to this early period.

In Dumfriesshire, at Rotten Bottom, a long-bow dating to between 4000 and 3600 was discovered under peat. It was made of yew-wood (**15**). Current orthodoxy is that yew was not growing in Scotland at this time; thus the bow is thought to be an import – whether exchanged with people from further south, or brought by an incomer. The leaf-shaped flint arrowheads of the Neolithic were fired from bows like this, which were capable of killing a deer or a person at short range.

At Lochhill, in Kirkcudbrightshire, a timber and stone mortuary house, quite like that at Pitnacree, was built during the first ten generations after 4000 (16). Massive D-shaped posts stood at either end of a rectilinear space outlined by granite boulders and fronted by a timber façade. There were two posts in the centre of the structure. The interior was floored with oak planks, and on the floor and among the overlying stones were small deposits of cremated bone. After it had been burnt down its remains were preserved because a wedge-shaped cairn, with a stone burial chamber at one end, was built over it; probably no great length of time passed before the cairn was built.

The west

Near Biggar a long barrow was built of earth, turf and stones dating within the first ten generations after 4000. The mound was nearly 4m (13ft) wide and 11–18m (37–60ft) long. This means it was right at the bottom end of the range of sizes known in Britain, for earthen long barrows are most commonly 30–60m (100–200ft) long, and can be 120m (400ft) long. Earthen long barrows, built of turf and soil, and sometimes covering a wooden chamber used for disposal of the dead, are among the most characteristic monuments of the fourth millennium in eastern Britain. Quite commonly, the wooden chambers were burnt down and it is generally assumed that this happened just before the mound was built. At Biggar Common, although there does not seem to have been a building burnt down just before mound-building started, bonfires of oak, hazel, birch and willow were lit just before work began. With the charcoal from these fires was found plain

round-bottomed Neolithic pottery and flint and chert tools. The underlying soil had been cultivated and we can be sure that there was Neolithic settlement nearby, perhaps a few hundred metres away where scatters of early Neolithic pottery have been discovered and excavation has recorded pits and post-holes.

At Monamore in Arran a bonfire was lit at some time during the first few centuries after 4000, in the area just in front of where a chambered tomb was to be built. Within a century or

16 *At Lochhill in south-western Scotland a timber and stone mortuary house was built 7.5m long by 1.4m wide (25 by nearly 5ft). It was built around massive posts. In its first phase it may have looked like the Pitnacree wicker box (see **14**). The lines of stones visible in the photograph may have been contemporary with the great posts, despite their similarity to those in the second-phase building at Pitnacree. Subsequently the building was covered by a chambered cairn.*

so of 3500, pits were dug at Machrie Moor in Arran, with fragments of plain round-bottomed bowls, in an area where timber and stone circles were later to be built. The lighting of fires at Biggar and Monamore presumably related to disposal of the dead rather than merely to clearance of the ground; and the deposition of broken pottery at Biggar and Machrie Moor also seems likely to have been part of a ritual.

Further west, oak was the dominant tree in the mixed woodlands of mainland Argyll south of Oban, except in the south of Kintyre and on higher ground, where birch was more common. Its coastal waters were probably as productive then as now, and mounds of shells attest to their exploitation both before and after 4000. No farming settlements, nor ritual sites, nor burials in Argyll are dated to the first ten generations after this date. During the following ten generations, however, a ritual monument and houses of considerable interest were built.

Temple Wood is in the Kilmartin valley, and today trees surround remains of a timber structure and two stone rings, together with later burials. The wood grows near to a string of five large burial cairns, and in the valley there are also alignments of standing stones and beautifully carved rock outcrops. The earliest of the cairns is a chambered tomb and under some of the other cairns Victorian excavators found what seem to be circular enclosures: in particular, under the northernmost or Glebe Cairn there was a double ring of stones comparable to the main stone ring at Temple Wood. However, despite the evidence for activities in the Kilmartin valley which may belong to this period, only Temple Wood has been radiocarbon dated.

The charred wood, and thus the date, probably relate to the timber structure, which was earlier then the stone rings. Its two deepest post-holes were respectively due north and due south of a central hollow, and since the depth of a post-hole is the best indication of the height of the posts (taller posts require deeper post-holes to be stable) it may be that these

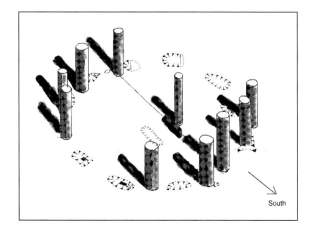

South

17 *At Temple Wood in the Kilmartin valley of western Scotland a timber structure was built. Its builders may have been intended it to be a ring about 10m (33ft) across. In the diagram posts are shown rising only from those holes where there was clear evidence for timbers. At the centre of the structure was a 1.65m (5½ft) long stone, pointing north–south, which rose only 0.5m (1½ft) above a cobbled surface. The timbers were replaced by stones, perhaps even before all the intended posts had been erected.*

were the most important elements of the timber setting (**17**). The excavator suggested that the timber structure, which may have been intended to be a ring, was never completed but was replaced by the overlying stone ring, which was built of fairly small slabs with a central stone, set on its long edge in a cobbled surface. It was aligned true north–south and cut the central post-hole of the timber structure.

The radiocarbon date has a larger uncertainty attached to it than most, and a health warning must be fixed to it since it is the only date from the early phases of the site. However, whether Temple Wood was of this period or dates between 3500 and 3000, the north–south alignment provides the earliest evidence from Scotland for careful observation of the movements of the sun. Such evidence need not occasion surprise. Farming communities required a good knowledge of the seasons, and a knowledge of true north, east, south and west was useful in tracking their changes. In this hilly area the simplest way to establish due south may have been to measure the direction of the shortest shadow cast by a post around midday, but the timber structure at Temple Wood was more complicated than it need have been for this purpose. It seems to show that rituals or ceremonies were bound up with seasonal cycles.

A stone, turf and stake-built house at Ardnadam near Dunoon in Argyll dates to the ten-generation period before 3500 (**18**). It was a round-cornered, straight-sided building with internal partitions and a central hearth. It was not the first on the site. A roughly oval house underlying it was succeeded nearby by a pair of houses or rooms and the corner of another house was found in the unexcavated area. The Neolithic pottery from the site was plain and of an early type. Ardnadam was a very significant discovery. It suggests that the early farmers of the west of Scotland lived in fairly small houses with straight sides and round corners, partitioned internally and built of turf, stone and poles.

An excavation at Newton on the island of Islay provides a good example of the difficulties of understanding the relationships between farmers and hunters. The first unambiguous evidence for people at Newton dates to just before 6500. At that time the sea was further away than it is today, and the area contained mixed open woodland of hazel, elm, birch and oak with perhaps some alder, bordering on an open freshwater loch. The settlement included a working hollow or small house, possibly with a pitched roof covering part of it. Local flint was used to make tools and hunting weapons. Most of the carbonized plant material from the site was hazelnut shells.

The excavation provided evidence for settlement in the period between 4000 and 3750, when there was some woodland clearance. It was followed by digging of pits and erection of fences, and pollen analysis suggests both arable and pastoral farming were firmly established by 3750–3500. The fences were lightly constructed, and they were repaired several times. Round-bottomed pottery of a classical early type was

found in the pits. The evidence fits well with the general model advocated in Chapter 1: non-intensive farming followed by creation of homeplots. At Newton, however, intensive agriculture was – perhaps after one or two generations – followed by a return of the land to pasture.

There are also dates for charcoal found with flints and animal bones, including sheep, under the chambered tomb at Port Charlotte on Islay.

18 *The radiocarbon-dated house at Ardnadam in Argyll, western Scotland, is the one marked 5 at the bottom left of this plan. It measured 3m (10ft) by, at the very least, 3m internally – the eastern part of the house could not be detected during excavation. To its north were found two roughly contemporary houses or rooms, the one marked 3 on this plan measuring internally about 4 by 3m (13 by 10ft) internally, and the one marked 4 measuring about 2.5 by 2m (8 by 6½ft). They were probably built on turf and stone foundations, and supported timber and turf roofs. There was plentiful evidence for several periods of reuse in the houses.*

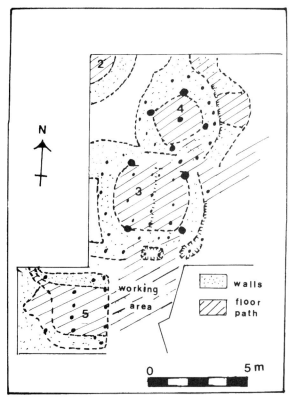

They suggest activity there at much the same time as pits were being dug at Newton. Yet although the evidence from Islay may seem to favour a sequence of hunter-gatherer use followed by an incursion of farmers many generations later, it does not provide any unambiguous proof; and indeed it is difficult to conceive what evidence other than biochemical testing of human bones could differentiate between developments among the hunters and the incoming of alien farmers.

The Western Isles

Around 4000 the Western Isles were mostly covered by rough pasture, with birch woodland in the eastern hills. In sheltered spots there were stands of Scots pine. The main constraint on agriculture was wind exposure. There is as yet no evidence for settlement until the centuries around 3500, when a small round-ended house was built on a hillside platform at Allt Chrysal on Barra, the southernmost of the large islands.

The spread of farming from 4000 to 3500

Farmers and hunters probably coexisted for ten generations or so after 4000, at least in the west. Food remains were discarded on shell middens on the Inner Hebrides and on a midden at Cardingmill Bay near Oban. Although the latter was disturbed by much later burials, and none of the parts of the middens dated to this period contained typical hunter-gatherer tools, they seem as likely to represent the old way of life as shellfish gathering by farmers. None of the shell midden mounds of the Forth valley have produced dates between 4000 and 3500, so perhaps the shellfish which formed the mounds were not exploited.

There is no evidence for intensive farming settlements north of Perthshire and Angus from 4000 to 3750. Archaeologists have speculated that the open ground of the western and

northern islands may have made them attractive for early farmers, but if they relied on exploitation of secondary forest it is possible that the sparsely wooded islands were not as attractive as previously supposed. Yet it is as likely that the lack of proof for settlement in the north reflects only the small number of modern excavations and the difficulties of distinguishing small houses and mounds of this period from those of others. Where there is evidence of settlement in the first ten generations after 4000, there are few signs of regional variations. If Scotland was still characterized by small populations with many long-distance networks, regional differences may have grown only slowly.

Evidence of settlement between 3750 and 3500 is found as far north as Caithness and the Western Isles (although there is still no direct evidence for farmers in Shetland, nor Orkney). The differences between regions after 3750 are very noticeable. Along with structures similar to those found in the first ten generations, the sites include distinctive chambered cairns and other burial places which fit into a long-lasting pattern of regional variation. In the north-east, in

19 *Air photography has recently revealed many timber and ditched structures which may date to between 4000 and 3000. All those shown here are from eastern Scotland except Holywood, which is in south-western Scotland. At the top are (from the left): Berryhill enclosure, with two entrances on the left side; Ardmuir pit-group, perhaps the remains of a structure including six posts; and four ditch segments at Sherriff Muir perhaps defining an enclosure or possibly edging a mound. The left centre picture shows the cursus at Holywood; notice that there are at least two gaps in each of the side ditches. At right centre is a similar shaped monument at Milton, but defined by lines of posts; there seem to be gaps at the end and on the right-hand side. Lastly, the roughly oval enclosure at Templeton seems to have an entrance in an in-curving façade at the upper end, as seen on this photograph. Maybe excavation will one day show that their dates range over an even longer period; but as a group they illustrate how varied, yet subtly related to each other, early farming traditions may have been on the Scottish lowlands.*

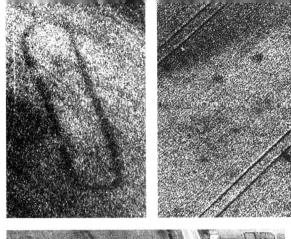
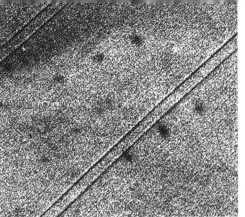

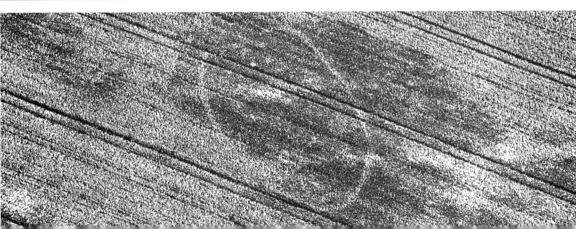

particular, there are hints that by 3500 a distinctive culture was developing. There is a possible social interpretation for these regional groupings. Weak long-distance kinship and gift-exchange contacts may have been supplemented or partially replaced by stronger, more local networks as both local populations and knowledge of local resources grew. On the other hand, the great timber building at Balbridie suggests direct links with the continental lowlands.

Apart from the unusually large hall at Balbridie, houses were probably small with straight sides and round corners. It seems likely that many people in the more fertile parts of the lowlands still exploited areas of secondary forest, clearing each plot of ground roughly every twenty years and then allowing it to return to forest after one or at most two croppings. Infield areas close to settlement were also being created. There is no direct evidence for what the infields looked like except at Newton on Islay where some were fenced; but they will have been small and intensively cultivated, probably by hand with wooden hoes or spades. In less fertile areas – perhaps particularly those near the top margin of the forest, but no doubt also in areas of poorer soil elsewhere – parts of the forest will have been turned to pasture by 3500. Very heavy clayey ground would probably not be suitable for early agriculture, and probably the people could not cope with boggy areas; but we probably underestimate the ability of these early farmers to exploit a wide range of soil and vegetation types both in the river valleys and on the uplands.

Probably the farmers just worked around large field stones, and smaller ones would be dumped in heaps or rough lines at the edge of agricultural plots. It is likely that sheep, goats and cattle were accompanied by herdsmen, whose duties would include pasture improvement, so pasture, too, was probably cleared of middle-sized surface stones.

Special places for disposal of the dead were created by all the communities of Scotland. The mortuary house and simple chambered cairn at Lochhill in the south-west seem likely to belong to the first ten generations after 4000, while the structures built in eastern Scotland at Pitnacree during the ten generations before 3500 may represent the same sequence in a slightly different form. The circular cremation area at Pitglassie suggests the tantalizing possibility that some of the supposedly later but undated stone circles which are so characteristic of the north-east derived from a tradition which started in this period (see Chapter 5). The abundance of cremations in burial places (albeit the burning of bones sometimes took place long after death and exposure of unburnt bodies in special places) is something of a surprise, but it may be due in part to the hazards of survival of evidence. Well-fired bone survives much better than unburnt bone in the acid soils so common in Scotland.

Ritual and ceremonial were probably deeply entwined with everyday living. Although the burial of broken pottery in pits may indicate the presence of settlements for which no other evidence survives, it is as likely that it symbolized some important aspect of life and death. Other structures may have been built explicitly for ceremonials (**19**). The bank barrow and ditches at the Cleaven Dyke have no utilitarian explanation, and the large timber enclosures at Inchtuthil and Douglasmuir may have been built for displays and dancing, bringing together the communities of the surrounding area. The timber structure at Temple Wood gives us another insight into the rituals and ceremonies of this period (although the health warning attached to the single date must not be forgotten), for it shows that people built measurements of the movements of the sun into their sacred places.

CHAPTER THREE

Regional diversity increases 3500 to 3000 BC

Selecting from traditions

In the twenty-generation period between 3500 and 3000 the climate was still somewhat warmer than it is today, and in general wetter; and despite a slight deterioration around 3250 the growing seasons would have been slightly longer and farming slightly easier than it is now. By 3500 pasture had replaced woodland around many settlements, but mountains, mires and the wild wood still separated communities. Except in north-east Scotland, which seems to have had distinctive burial practices, the differences between regions stemmed from variations within a broad cultural uniformity; it seems communities were each selecting from a common set of appropriate responses to death and the problems of living.

The distinctions between regions became stronger as time passed until about 3000, when social changes associable with new forms of pottery occurred, coinciding with a strengthening of links between distant places. Archaeologists have conjectured that around and after 3000 power was increasingly concentrated in a few hands, and that new types of structure and prestigious objects were signs of the rise of chieftains. These matters will be reviewed, and discussion extended beyond the radiocarbon-dated sites, after descriptions of the sites and objects dated to this period (**20**).

Shetland

Evidence from pollen analysis shows there had been some clearance of birch and hazel scrub on Shetland before now, and about 3500 a field wall was built at Shurton, near Lerwick. There are signs of more long-lasting clearance during the next generations. Grassland spread, and areas near a settlement at Scord of Brouster, in West Shetland, were cultivated.

Round about the middle of this period a small house was built at Scord of Brouster. It was found below a stone building, and no definite information about its shape or size was discovered during excavation. It is possible that it was built of turf and wood, for there was pasture nearby and trees grew in sheltered spots. A small stone bead shows it is likely that the soapstone outcrops of the island were already exploited by about 3250.

Shetland is visible from Fair Isle, which is in turn in sight of Orkney. It is tempting to think that settlement reached Shetland from Orkney. However, Shetland developed a distinctive regional character over the next few centuries. Almost all of its chambered cairns are heel-shaped. It may be (since heel-shaped cairns are not known in Orkney but, as we saw in Chapter 2, one was built at Tulach an t'Sionnaich in Caithness shortly after 3500) that the Shetlands were settled from Caithness or even further south. Logboats, birch-bark canoes or skin curraghs or coracles would allow movement of

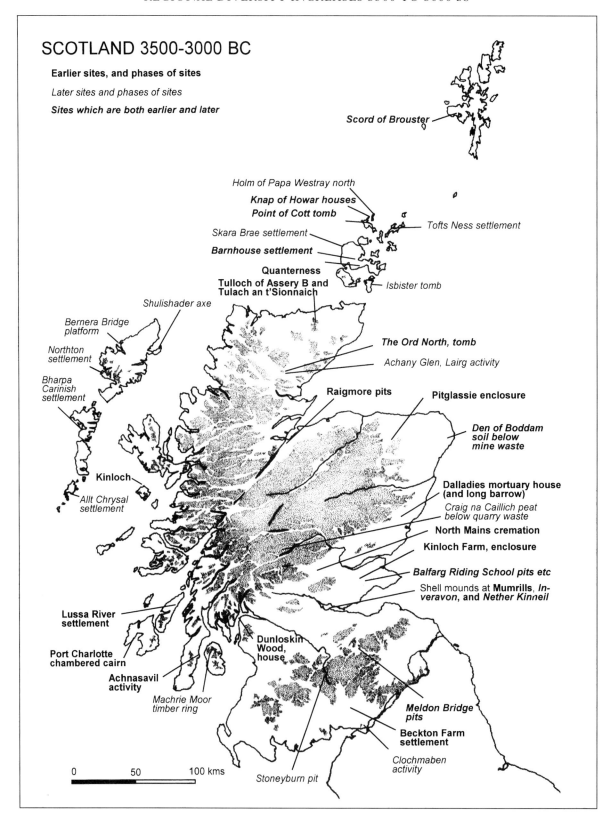

SCOTLAND 3500-3000 BC

Earlier sites, and phases of sites

Later sites and phases of sites

Sites which are both earlier and later

Scord of Brouster

Holm of Papa Westray north
Knap of Howar houses
Point of Cott tomb
Skara Brae settlement
Tofts Ness settlement
Barnhouse settlement
Quanterness
**Tulloch of Assery B and
Tulach an t'Sionnaich**
Isbister tomb

Shulishader axe

*Bernera Bridge
platform*

The Ord North, tomb

Achany Glen, Lairg activity

*Northton
settlement*

*Bharpa
Carinish
settlement*

Raigmore pits

Pitglassie enclosure

***Den of Boddam
soil below
mine waste***

Kinloch

*Allt Chrysal
settlement*

**Dalladies mortuary house
(and long barrow)**

*Craig na Caillich peat
below quarry waste*

North Mains cremation

Kinloch Farm, enclosure

Balfarg Riding School pits etc

Shell mounds at **Mumrills**, *Inveravon*, and *Nether Kinneil*

**Lussa River
settlement**

**Dunloskin
Wood,
house**

**Port Charlotte
chambered cairn**

**Achnasavil
activity**

*Machrie Moor
timber ring*

***Meldon Bridge
pits***

**Beckton Farm
settlement**

*Clochmaben
activity*

Stoneyburn pit

0   50   100 kms

20 *Map of sites radiocarbon dated to between 3500 and 3000.*

people and goods between distant places long known to the hunter-gatherers. A short period of initial settlement of both archipelagos from the mainland may explain what we see better than gradual island hopping.

Orkney

The vegetation of Orkney, like that of Shetland, was dominated by a mixture of grassland and birch and hazel scrub. Recent finds of flints typical of the hunter-gatherers suggest people had lived there for many generations, and grassland had become more abundant over the two or three centuries preceding 3500. It is difficult to tell whether the scrub was cleared by hunters or farmers, but the latter probably reached Orkney before or around this time since the houses and chambered cairns which have been dated to the next ten generations show a considerable mastery of building techniques. The Orkney flagstones are very suitable for building, but taking into account the similarity of the pottery of this period to that of farmers further south, it seems more likely that some of them brought their constructional skills to Orkney than that local hunter-gatherers learnt new skills.

The two stone houses at Knap of Howar (**colour plate 2**), on the western shore of the small island of Papa Westray, were set into a midden of animal bones and shells which started to accumulate around or a few generations after 3500. The buildings found during excavation were not part of the earliest occupation in the area (since they were set into midden) but the midden underlying the buildings and the midden contemporary with their use contained similar graceful round-bottomed bowls with incised decoration, and there seems little reason to suppose there was a long break in occupation before the houses were built at some time in this period.

The middens provide evidence of a varied diet. They contained barley, and remains of cattle, sheep and pigs with lesser amounts of wild animal bones, especially those of deer, seals and whales. Wheat pollen was found nearby. There were also the bones of many birds, including both summer and winter visitors, so clearly the site was occupied all year round. The many fish remains included species which were most probably caught by line fishing between two and five miles offshore. Many limpets were found in the middens; they may have been used for bait, but other species were probably collected for eating. Oysters were fairly common and some winkles and cockles were found. There were a few examples each of many other kinds of shellfish, some of which may have been collected for decoration.

No wood, plant fibres, or leather survive, so we know little, for instance, about what people wore. There was, however, a wide range of tools made of bone and stone for cutting, boring, piercing, scraping and pounding; they are evidence for leatherworking, but not for manufacture of cloth (**21**).

A chambered cairn was built on Holm of Papa Westray some time before 3000. The Holm may have been connected to Papa Westray during this period, and pieces of bowls like those from Knap of Howar were discovered at the chambered cairn; so perhaps the people who lived at Knap of Howar buried their dead here. The cairn was small and rectangular; the chamber inside occupied a large proportion of it (**22**). Entered by a passage at the north-west end, the main chamber was divided up into four compartments by vertical slabs projecting from the sides of the chamber. At its inner end was a small trapezoidal cell inside its own roughly built supporting cairn. This innermost cell was carefully packed with layers of stones, deer tines, shells, animal, fish and human bones some time after 3000. Subsequently the main chamber was altered slightly, so this packing took place while the tomb was still in use.

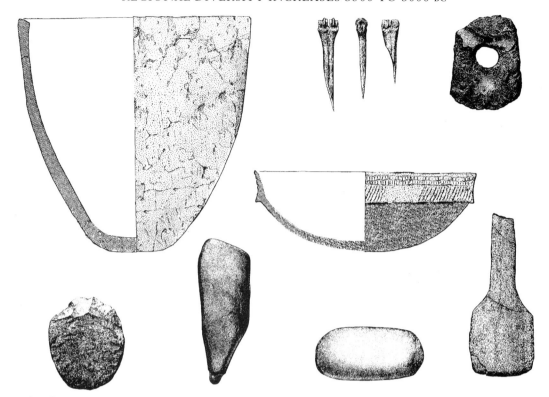

21 *The illustration shows a small part of the tool-kit used by the farmers at Knap of Howar in Orkney (see **colour plate 2**). All are shown at (approximately) the same scale, and the large storage pot was about 0.3m (1ft) across. It and the graceful drinking bowl are similar to vessels found in chambered tombs like Point of Cott and Holm of Papa Westray North. The bone awls at top centre were used for piercing leather. The bone macehead (top right) may have been used to drive in pegs to stretch animal skins, or for flintworking. Large pebble flake knives like that at bottom left were used for cutting. Stone borers, many smaller than that shown, were used with a sand abrasive to make holes in antler and stone. The stone pounder may have been used to crush seeds or pigments. The whale-bone spatula (bottom right) would not have been out of place in a modern kitchen. In addition there were many other pots, and flint, stone, bone and antler tools for cutting, piercing, pounding embossing, grinding, and other tasks. Other parts of the tool-kit, made of wood, animal skin or fibres, have not survived.*

Remains of several burials were found in the main chamber, together with plain graceful pottery bowls.

The large chambered tomb at Point of Cott on Westray is not very distant from Knap of Howar, across the water. The burial chamber was a neater, more spacious version of the chamber at Holm of Papa Westray North and it too was immediately surrounded by a small nearly rectangular cairn, which was probably constructed to hold down the back ends of corbelling stones forming the chamber walls (**23**). Between this and the exterior of the final cairn were several internal strengthening walls. In its final form the cairn was similar in shape to some of the Caithness cairns, with a long body and horns projecting to either side of the entrance passage leading to the chamber. Both human and animal bones were found inside the chamber. Like all the chambered cairns discussed so far, it seems to have been reverenced for many centuries: infant burials were inserted into the cairn at a much later period. All the animal bones have much later dates than the human bones, and the excavator has suggested that carnivores, possibly feral dogs and birds of prey, sheltered there after it was abandoned by people.

22 *The chambered cairn at Holm of Papa Westray North in Orkney was less than 12m (40ft) long by just over 6m (20ft) wide. It was the smaller of at least two tombs on the island. The photograph shows its neat façade and entrance passage, and upright slabs can just be seen dividing up the chamber beyond.*

At some time during the ten generations before 3000 a large chambered tomb was built at Isbister, in South Ronaldsay, at the other end of Orkney. It was different in plan from Point of Cott, because in addition to vertical stones dividing the central chamber into compartments

23 *The chambered cairn at Point of Cott on Westray in Orkney was at least 30m (roughly 100ft) long; the sea eroded its northern end and eastern side before it was measured accurately. The chamber inside was 8.2m (27ft) long. The diagram shows the outside of the main burial vault, constructed by overlapping each successively higher stone inward from the one supporting it. It may have had vertical outer faces rather than the curved ones shown here. The entrance passage was roofed with large slabs. The business part of the tomb was encased in stone walls, the outer of which curved out at the end as shown on the right-hand side. The incurving façade is not shown on this diagram.*

it had side cells entered from the main chamber, and the cairn was oval (**24**). However, the pottery in it included shallow graceful round-bottomed bowls decorated like those from Point of Cott and Knap of Howar. The tomb contained almost as wide a variety of animal and plant remains as the middens at Knap of Howar, probably because domestic rubbish was put into the tomb. The human skeletons, only parts of which were found in the tomb, had been exposed elsewhere; but a few articulated sets of bones suggested that the skeletons were complete until shortly before parts of them were put in the chamber. Different body parts, like skulls and long bones, had at some stage been collected into separate groups, suggesting that at some stage these people revered their ancestors as a group rather than as individuals.

24 *The chambered cairn at Isbister had been damaged by waves before it was excavated, although it stood at the top of 30m (roughly 100ft) sea-cliffs. Its original shape is unknown, but the outer rubble cairn was over 30m (roughly 100ft) across. The chamber was 8.2m (27ft) long, and divided into five compartments by tall vertical slabs. The two end ones had stone shelves about 1.2–1.4m (4–5ft) above the floor. In addition the tomb had three side cells, each about 1m (3ft) tall, of which one can be seen in the foreground of this photograph.*

Many of those buried in Isbister died young. The male life expectancy at the age of 15 was about 13 years, while that of women was only 9 years, presumably because many died in child-birth. At an average 1.7m (5ft 7in) tall, the men were some 0.1m (3in) shorter than today's generation, and the women were on average 1.6m (5ft 3in) tall. The bones showed signs of hard work, including the carrying of heavy loads. Accidental injuries included crushed vertebrae of the kind caused by long falls, but there were no signs of personal violence. Perhaps some people were injured climbing down the cliffs of South Ronaldsay in search of birds and their eggs. It was a society in which everyone worked hard, and there was no leisured class.

Occupation of a stone house at Tofts Ness on Sanday began towards 3000. Only part of it was excavated, and it had been damaged by later structures. It contained two successive central hearths, and slots with packing for stone uprights indicated that it contained stone furniture. The pottery from it and the middens to either side was plain.

The radiocarbon-dated evidence we have seen so far suggests very small settlements of one or two houses. At the very least a century before 3000, however, there was a change. New kinds of pottery were made (**25**). Some

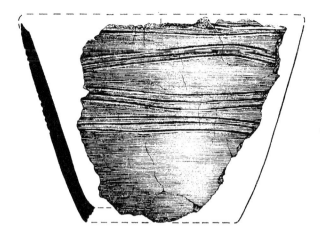

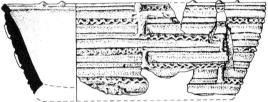

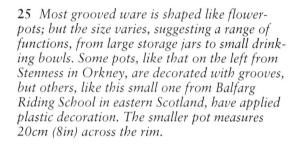

pots were large, coarse and designed for storage while others were small and fine enough to serve as drinking bowls. Archaeologists call all these kinds of pottery grooved ware. The importance of grooved ware lies partly in its discovery at many ceremonial sites throughout Britain. It was also used at a settlement of several houses at Barnhouse, where the brackish Loch of Stenness and the freshwater Loch of Harray meet in the main island.

The houses at Barnhouse varied in shape from oval to straight sided with round corners. They were built of stone and turf, and had turf roofs. Inside the ordinary houses a central rectangular hearth was flanked on both sides by box beds recessed into the walls and large enough for several people to sleep in (26); at the rear of each house was a stone dresser. Outside each house was a spread of ashes and burnt bones.

The village was highly organized. All of the houses had stone-built drains which fed out into ditches running down to the Loch of Harray. The hearths were all oriented in much the same direction. When houses were replaced (one of them as many as five times over the centuries) the basic plan of the village was retained. They surrounded an open area in which people made flint tools, fired pots, and worked bone and hides (the evidence for this was the pumice used for abrading and smoothing bones and animal skins). Each industry had its own favoured spot within the open space.

25 *Most grooved ware is shaped like flowerpots; but the size varies, suggesting a range of functions, from large storage jars to small drinking bowls. Some pots, like that on the left from Stenness in Orkney, are decorated with grooves, but others, like this small one from Balfarg Riding School in eastern Scotland, have applied plastic decoration. The smaller pot measures 20cm (8in) across the rim.*

26 *The ordinary houses in the settlement at Barnhouse in Orkney were about 5m (16½ft) long internally. Most were roughly oval externally. The remains of several can be seen in the background of this excavation photograph. House 2, in the foreground, was double-sized. The nearer half was poorly preserved, although its hearth can still be seen. The more distant half preserves the shape of the bedchambers better, arrayed round the other hearth. Like the other houses, its neat rectilinear interior contrasts with its rounded exterior.*

House 2, a double-sized structure, was built to a much better standard than the small houses, and although its external wall-faces had rounded corners, its internal wall-faces were straight. In its two internal compartments it had in all six bed recesses. The polished stone tools found in it were made to a better standard than those in other houses and it may have been used for the manufacture of mace-heads and carved stone balls. There are many possible explanations as to why it was different from the other buildings; if archaeologists are correct in their conjecture that this period saw a rise of chieftains, the house may have belonged to the most important person in the village. Alternatively, although the alternatives are not mutually exclusive, it may have been used for cult practices, for that might explain the making of special ceremonial objects.

From this period, just before 3000, there are also the first dates from the earliest levels at Skara Brae, that famous settlement on the west coast of Orkney. The pottery used there was grooved ware. There is no clear evidence that even the earliest houses visible today had been built. But settlements with grooved-ware pottery, which is found at so many important sites in Britain, were well established on the mainland of Orkney at least several generations before 3000.

It may be that the people who used grooved ware also constructed chambered tombs around this time, because there are two dates of this period from a tomb containing grooved ware at Quanterness, not far from Barnhouse. One date was from a skeleton which seems to

27 *This excavation plan and cross-section show the nature of the chambered tomb at Quanterness, in Orkney, which was 31m (over 100ft) in diameter and contained a chamber measuring 6.4 by 1.8m (21 by 6ft) and originally 3.5m (nearly 12ft) tall. Its side chambers varied in size, averaging around 3m (10ft) long by 2.5m (8ft) tall.*

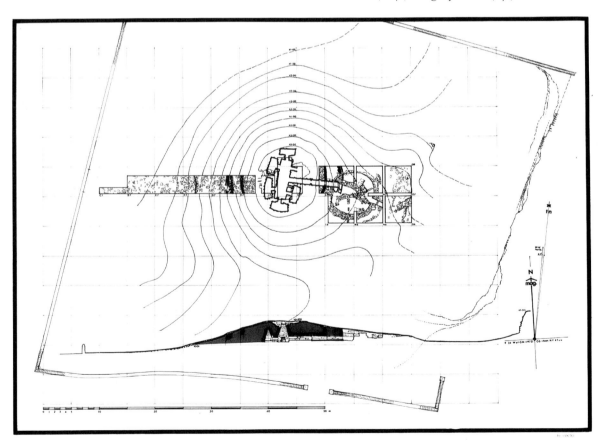

have been among the first put in the main chamber. The cairn was circular, with internal revetment walls. The main chamber was at the centre of the cairn and took the form of an undivided hall. It was entered by a long side passage, and six large cells were reached from the hall through narrow passages (27). As in many Caithness tombs, the chamber contents included whole skeletons at base and top separated by a jumbled mass of bones and domestic rubbish.

Point of Cott, with its round-bottomed bowls, and Quanterness, with its grooved ware, represent two extremes among the chambered cairns of Orkney. In many ways Isbister represents a hybrid form. Point of Cott seems to be the earliest, followed by Isbister and then Quanterness. This need not imply a neat progression from the Point of Cott type of tomb to the Quanterness type; it shows rather that the people of these three different parts of Orkney gave emphasis to different parts of a common tradition, and suggests that the tombs with grooved ware were a local development.

The north

Apart from use of the tombs at Tulach an t'Sionnaich and Tulloch of Assery B, discussed in Chapter 2, there is no radiocarbon-dated evidence for settlements or burials in Caithness or north-west Sutherland during the twenty generations between 3500 and 3000. By now, no doubt, the birch forest had been turned to pasture and small infields in many areas.

At The Ord, a hill just to the south-west of Lairg in Sutherland, there is a cairn covering a passage and chamber (28). It was most probably built at some time during the ten-generation period after 3500. As at other places, the chambered cairn was used for disposal of the dead for many centuries, perhaps forty generations of people in this case. The shallow round-bottomed Neolithic bowls that archaeologists have learnt to expect at tombs of this period in northern Scotland were indeed found; but so was a wide

28 *The chambered tomb at The Ord, Lairg, in northern Scotland, was heart-shaped and measured about 22.5m (74ft) by 29m (95ft). The chamber and passage are shown during excavation. The chamber was 13m (42ft) long and divided into two compartments. The passage, over 4m (about 14ft) long, was divided into two roughly equal parts by two large vertical stones.*

range of other pots including a globular bowl combining incised and impressed decoration; this probably reflects the length of time over which the chamber was used rather than a diversity in contemporary pottery styles. The latest burials were cremations along with small flat-bottomed pots characteristic of the period after 2000. Again, as at other places, the cairn was enlarged at some time, blocking and covering up the entrance to the passage; but here the enlargement left a roughly round cairn, not a long cairn.

In Achany Glen, just south of Lairg on what is today a bleak heather-covered moor, excavation has turned up a large assemblage of pottery from buried agricultural soils. The pots were similar to those found under a field dyke, and under a cairn in a pit, dating between 3250 and 3000. Although later prehistoric agriculture had removed any evidence which may have existed for buildings of this period in the areas excavated, the soils testify to widespread agriculture during the period that the nearby chambered tomb at The Ord was in use.

The north-east and east

On Deeside the great timber hall at Balbridie was burnt down, probably at some time between 3500 and 3250. It is difficult to see

29 *Over 450 mine-shafts are visible as hollows in the ground at Den of Boddam, near Peterhead in north-eastern Scotland. They cut through barren material to reach layers of flint pebbles, and some were as much as 3.5m (11ft) deep. The diagram shows the cross-section of a long-abandoned mine, a mine in use and a recently abandoned one being filled with a succession of layers of debris. In the background are mounds of waste material from other pits.*

any long-lasting influence from the direct contact which Balbridie demonstrates between the continent and this area, and it looks as if the people concentrated on local contacts. However, towards 3000 a local flint industry developed in north-east Scotland which is most comparable to industries in East Anglia, southern England and the continent.

One shaft of the extraordinary flint-mining site at Den of Boddam near Peterhead (**29**) is loosely dated to the centuries around 3000 by a radiocarbon date from soil buried by its spoil. It seems unlikely that archaeologists have by chance hit on the earliest, but the flint was probably exploited mostly in the first part of the next millennium. The pits were dug deep through glacial till to a layer with flint cobbles. Once abandoned they filled up quickly, for the till was unstable. Each one represents a considerable amount of work, which shows that good-quality flint was of high value. It seems quite likely that it was not all made into tools and weapons by the miners; some of it will have been traded or exchanged. However, there

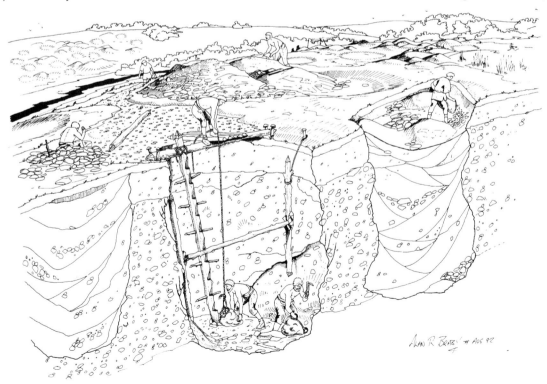

are other sources of similar red, brown or yellow flint in eastern Scotland and only when many flints have been chemically analysed will it be possible to build up a pattern of dispersal.

A small timber structure for disposal of the dead was built further south, in Kincardineshire, around the middle of this period. It was discovered beneath Dalladies earthen long barrow, and was similar to the mortuary houses at Lochhill in south-west Scotland and at Pitnacree in Perthshire, both of which were described in Chapter 2. The first structure was post-built, possibly a slighter version of those at Pitnacree and Lochhill. It was replaced by a rectangular enclosure defined by stone banks, with an elaborate entrance of earth and timber. It seems that the structure was roofed with birch-bark, but there were no signs of any vertical structural timbers. It was burnt down just before the long barrow was built. Thus although the mortuary house may have stood for a long time it seems most likely that the barrow too was built around the middle of this period (30).

The barrow was built of turf revetted with stone walls; horns swept out to either side at the east end. It may have been built to assert the social importance and the grazing and planting rights of the community. The large amount of turf used in its construction implies abundant local pasture. This suggests in turn that the people who built Dalladies had turned to the use of rip ploughs pulled by draught animals. Ploughs would be almost essential if their fields returned to pasture during fallow periods, and abundant pasture meant that draught animals could be fed on the grasslands rather than requiring up to half of a planted cereal crop for their own sustenance.

Further to the south and west, an axehead quarry at Creag na Caillich in Perthshire was exploited by small, individual groups who

30 *The space enclosed by the second (radiocarbon dated) mortuary structure at Dalladies in north-eastern Scotland was about 6.5m (22ft) long and 2m (6–7ft) wide. Two posts at the entrance left a gap 0.4m (slightly over 1½ft) wide. The turf barrow which covered it was over 50m (165ft) long. Here the mortuary house is shown during excavation, and the neatly sectioned remains of the turf mound loom over the excavators.*

travelled to the site to collect their own stone. This suggests that although finer stone axeheads might be traded or exchanged over considerable distances, they did not satisfy all local needs. It may be that the quarry at Craig na Caillich, like the flint-mines at Den of Boddam, was used predominantly in the next period, for it is only loosely dated from peat growing below and above one of the chipping floors where the axehead rough-outs were made.

At North Mains in Perthshire near an area where, later, a ceremonial timber circle and earthwork were built (see Chapter 4), animal bones were buried in a pit cut by a later ring ditch which itself probably defined an area for disposal of the dead. Perhaps this represents a variation on the ideas represented by the burying of broken pottery in pits.

The roughly circular enclosure at Kinloch Farm, Collessie, Fife was first detected as a superficially uninspiring site on an air photograph. Only a very small part of it was dug, the material used for the radiocarbon date was not ideal, and the pottery was unlike that found at other sites known to belong to the period between 3500 and 3000. It was plain, with flat rims and is most easily compared to vessels found throughout Scotland and dated to between 1750 and 1000. Archaeology is full of stories of sites which appeared, when first found, to be incompatible with the accepted models of the past; and perhaps Collessie represents yet another aspect of regional diversity. Yet at much the same time broken pots of types more normally found on sites dated to this period were being buried at Balfarg Riding School. For the moment it seems best to suppose that the radiocarbon evidence at Collessie comes from charcoal much earlier than the round enclosure and the pottery.

There are several dates for the Forth valley shell middens at Inveravon, Mumrills and Nether Kinneil. Oyster shells had been deposited on some of the mounds before 4500, and they were to continue in use until after 2000. It is curious that we have no radiocarbon

dates from them showing use in the period immediately before this one, for hunting and gathering of food were parts of the strategies of farmers, who will have found the oyster beds of the Forth valley a reliable and readily accessible source of food.

The south

Further south, at Meldon Bridge, by Peebles, there was activity in the two or three centuries before 3000 on what was, many generations later, to be the interior of a large, irregular defended enclosure. Pits were dug, containing and in some cases lined with broken pottery. In the only part of the site which had been protected from heavy ploughing there were traces of gullies which may have been the last signs of a settlement of shallowly founded timber houses. Perhaps, however, the pits were dug for ritual burial of pottery, animal bones or burnt material, as archaeologists have suggested for pits at North Mains and Balfarg Riding School.

A newly discovered and apparently long-lived settlement at Beckton, near Lockerbie, consisted of small houses built of stakes and floored with clay. There is one date from the earlier part of this period for a hearth sealed between clay floors. The settlement continued in occupation until well after 3000. Very little pottery was recovered from the site; and what was retrieved seems to belong to later phases of settlement. Beckton is reminiscent of the small cluster of houses at Ardnadam in Argyll described in Chapter 2, in that it is difficult to tell whether more than one or two buildings were in use at any one time.

The west

At Stoneyburn in Clydesdale a pit with Neolithic pottery under one of three small flat cairns provides another possible explanation for the pits which speckle the ground in areas in which large ritual and burial structures were to be built. Similar small earth and turf mounds covering token deposits would not long survive the ploughs of the medieval and later periods. In Argyll, the chambered tomb at Port Charlotte in Islay had been built on top of the flint and animal-bone debris which had strewn the site. The radiocarbon date, implying a true date before 3250, comes from charcoal left by a fire lit against one of the side stones of the chamber. There is also more evidence for settlement in Argyll. At Dunloskin Wood, a hearth found at the centre of a lightly built oval house, 9.5m (32ft) across, has been dated to this period. That said, it was the hearth rather than the post-holes which was dated and it may be that it went with a straight-sided, round-cornered house built of turf, hints of which the excavators recorded. Nevertheless, it potentially adds yet another element of diversity to our picture of settlement in the Neolithic and it warns us that types of structure which are usually assumed to be much later may occur quite early on, before 3250.

The Western Isles

In the Western Isles there is continuing evidence for activity at the settlement on the hillside platform at Allt Chrysal on Barra. Indeed, at Allt Chrysal we have evidence so far unique in Scotland: a surviving turf or peat clamp containing an unfired Neolithic pot. What few studies have been done suggest that most Neolithic pottery was locally made, but at Allt Chrysal we have direct proof.

At Bharpa Carinish on North Uist, close to a chambered cairn, a small settlement started towards the end of this period. The pottery from it included round-bottomed bowls like those found in Orkney and much of northern Scotland in this period and also vessels in more local styles. Within an area less than 5m long by 2m wide (17 by 6ft) were post-holes, shallow pits, three neat stone-lined hearths, charcoal and ash. The excavator argued that the remains probably represent successive houses with turf or earth walls, pointing to

accounts of building methods used in the Western Isles in recent times and to other archaeological sites where houses seem to have been built of turf and earth.

Some idea of the potential richness of Neolithic diets can be gained from the results of excavation at Northton in Harris. No permanent structures were discovered in Neolithic levels, and we may suppose the site represents but one aspect of the economy of the people who used it. The remains discovered here included crabs and lobsters, shellfish (predominantly cockles, implying extensive sand or mud flats nearby), seals and whales, and both juvenile and mature sheep and cattle, implying lamb, mutton, veal and beef. Among the remains were abundant potsherds similar to those at Bharpa Carinish.

An axe found in peat at Shulishader, Lewis has been dated to this period (**31**). The single-piece wooden axe haft had an oval socket into which was fixed a stone axehead, possibly made out of Antrim porcellanite. If it was made of Antrim stone it is also the first directly dated evidence for long-distance trade or gift exchange. It seems likely also, although the dating evidence comes from a pollen column rather than direct from the site, that there were agricultural fields near Calanais well before 3000. Excavation at Calanais itself led to the

31 *This complete and beautifully carved axe was found at Shulishader, on Lewis in the Western Isles, in a peat cutting. Its head was made of porcellanite, probably from Antrim in Northern Ireland.*

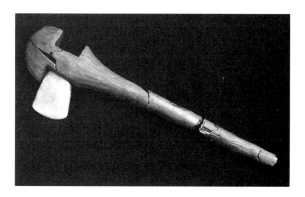

discovery of as yet undated agricultural ridges where later the great cruciform stone setting was built (see **colour plate** 7).

Seeds of greatness

There was increasing regional diversity with time. The characteristic way of disposing of the dead in the north and west of Scotland, including the island groups, seems to have been burial in chambered cairns. In the north-east and east earthen long barrows may by this period have served as expressions of local power, sealing earlier places in which bones were laid out. In the north-east (and perhaps further south) a rather different set of customs was developing, the depositing of cremations inside circular areas defined by upright posts or stones.

Although they are largely confined to the north and west, chambered cairns should provide one of the best ways of describing the differences and similarities between regions. For instance, in south-west Scotland the chambers had no passage, and they were divided into compartments by horizontal cross-slabs set in the floor. In Caithness and Orkney, in tombs which often had long passages, a very similar effect was achieved inside the chamber by vertical slabs set in the walls. It is tempting to think that timber and turf equivalents existed in Strathtay and elsewhere; strong bracing-timbers used to create a large wooden box lined with wattle and turf might look rather like the vertical and horizontal slab-dividers found in the stone-built tombs. Be this as it may, differences in construction may hide a great similarity in ritual and purpose. Until we have far more dates for both complex and simple chambered tombs, detailed typological schemes are more likely to lead us astray than help to sort out what the tombs meant to the people who built them. That said, there are broad types which each seem to occur much more in one area than others, although there was considerable diversity within each area, and tombs most characteristic of one area are found in others.

The impression gained from looking at the detail underlying the map (32) is that for most of the period between 4000 and 2500 each community which built a chambered cairn dipped into a bag of varied traditions and rituals. At first, perhaps, there was not much innovation: the idea of chambered tombs was adopted without much local variation by farmers who had started to practise intensive agriculture near their settlements. These small groups probably built fairly small tombs, and it is tempting to speculate that simple tombs represent a rapid early spread of a set of ideas among existing communities; but it is equally possible that some of them belong to the period between 3500 and 3000 and represent difference in choice of ritual or of the size of the community they served. Increasingly, after 3500, suitable spouses could be found in the local area, and gift exchange or barter within a set of local communities could supply most needs. Chambered tombs became more elaborate to satisfy a larger local population and to demonstrate the power of the community among its neighbours. That said, the axehead from Shulishader proves that some long-distance exchange took place, if only in prestigious objects.

There was increased clearance of the ancient forest, and at the same time the areas which had never been more than lightly forested, and those which were much more suited to pasture than woodland, were broken in by farmers; but there was everywhere a continued reliance on wild resources. In the generally milder climate

32 *Over the period 4000 to 2500 particular types of burial chamber (and distinctive types of covering mound) were favoured in different areas. This map shows a simplified version of their distribution and that of long cairns with no stone chambers. The intention is to show where the types have been discovered, rather than how many there were. Thus one symbol may represent very few or many tombs. The details of some tombs are masked by their cairns, and nearly every year more tombs are discovered. In addition, we know some tombs have been destroyed. The overall pattern, however, is fairly reliable.*

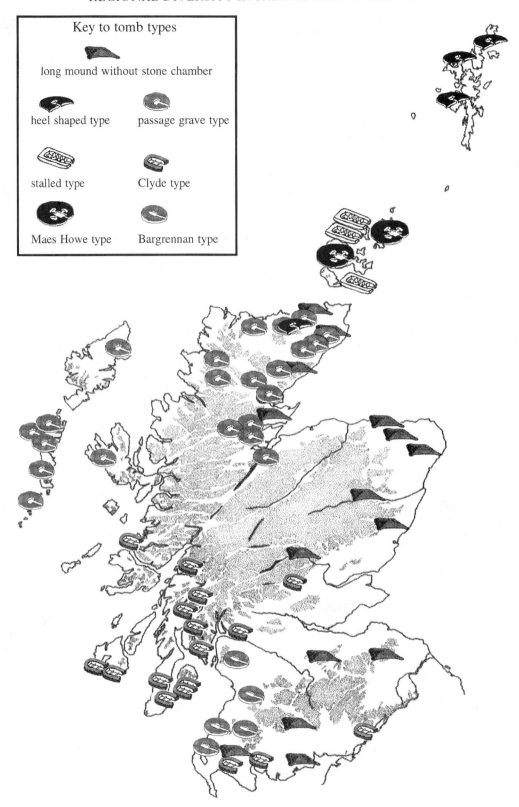

Key to tomb types

long mound without stone chamber

heel shaped type

passage grave type

stalled type

Clyde type

Maes Howe type

Bargrennan type

of the period, communities had rich and varied diets. Wild animals, birds, fish and shellfish formed part of the diet, but cattle, sheep and pigs were (generally in that order) more important supplies of protein. Wheat and barley were grown and the roots, fruits and seeds of wild plants were gathered. Intensive agriculture and increasing amounts of pasture made it sensible to keep draught animals to help plough the land and to manure the infield, and this in turn led to a requirement for still more pasture.

At the beginning of the period houses seem to have been isolated or in very small settlements, like Ardnadam. There was probably a strong tradition of building in turf in the west; but the evidence is ambiguous, and a site on Eilean Domhnuill in North Uist suggests that robbing of stones to build new structures may be a better explanation for the absence of neat wall lines at other sites. Although the settlement there has not been radiocarbon dated, the pottery in it suggests that it was occupied some time between 4000 and 3000. It was built on a small island in Loch Olabhat connected to the shore by a causeway. A succession of occupations suggests it was used for many generations. The houses were straight sided and round cornered; their stone-faced walls were packed with rubble and earth. However, many of the buildings had been dismantled, leaving only their floors, their neatly kerbed and paved hearths and traces of the house walls. The excavator's interpretation is that the island held only one substantial house at any one time (33). When a new house was built, it was to one side of the existing house and the material of the earlier house was used for building the new one.

Before 3000, little villages with one house more important than the others appeared, at least at Barnhouse in Orkney. They can be interpreted as support for the idea that society changed around this time. Perhaps land-hunger had led some families to work for others. Perhaps people who had concentrated on

33 *This reconstruction view of settlement on Eilean Domhnuill, Loch Olabhat, on North Uist in the Western Isles, shows a dwelling house, another building and animal pens. Most of the time there was only one house – each one was robbed of its stone to build its successor. During the period of occupation of the island the houses varied in internal size from 5 to 7m (16 to 23ft) long and 3 to 4.5m (10 to 15ft) wide.*

pastoralism for several generations took over power within agricultural communities. Both mechanisms for change have occurred frequently in other parts of the world as local populations grew beyond the capacity of existing social systems to absorb new demands for farming-land. Barnhouse has another significance for us. It was built on top of the old ground surface with stone, turf and clay, rather than with deeply dug post-holes. Had a similar settlement been built anywhere in the heavily ploughed agricultural lands of Scotland, what could we expect to survive? Another excavation, at Beckton near Lockerbie in Dumfriesshire, gives us part of an answer. It too contained grooved ware (although of the period after 3000); but apart from a few stake-holes, hearths and spreads of a clay reminiscent of that used in the construction of some of the Barnhouse houses, what survived from this period were pits. More generally, if most of the Neolithic houses in Scotland were built of turf, small stones and light poles, all we would expect to recover today would be the pits and the deeper post-holes. Perhaps the Neolithic pits at Douglasmuir, Raigmore, Meldon Bridge and Balfarg Riding School are the remnants of long-lived settlements of lightly built houses.

It was probably mostly in this millennium that rock outcrops were first marked with complex designs (34), although it is quite possible that the hunter-gatherers of earlier periods were responsible for some of them, for none of them are radiocarbon dated. However, a simply decorated stone was found in the mound at Dalladies and stones with more complex ornament were built into sites dated to between 3000 and 2000. Of the very many explanations proffered for these decorated outcrops, the best-argued is that they were territorial markers. They are most common in the west and south-west, where careful analysis of their positions has shown they were sited to give good views (and thus their positions, although not the rocks themselves, would have been readily visible).

34 *At Achnabreck, in the Kilmartin valley of Argyll in Western Scotland, there are three main groups of carvings. The photograph shows one small but fairly typical part of the largest group, which forms the greatest concentration of carvings known in the British Isles. The carvings include lines and hollows, like small cups, surrounded by single or multiple rings, some with lines cutting across their circuits. The group to which the carvings shown here belong includes a double spiral like a ram's horns.*

There is evidence for four different ways in which polished stone axes and other stone tools were obtained in Scotland: through trade or gift exchange with Ireland and northern England (for many axes made of stone from Great Langdale in the Lake District have been found in Scotland); and by exploiting quarries, flint-mines and stray stones or pebbles. The overall impression is that, despite a continuing gentle deterioration in the climate, people were prosperous, and in the next period we shall see how this prosperity was translated into great monuments. With hindsight, given what was to occur in the next twenty generations, the imported Shulishader axehead may suggest a new demand for prestigious objects, individual symbols of power. Nevertheless, when change did come to some communities, as with the adoption of grooved ware, it did not lead to a replacement of old practices in other communities. Instead, at least in Orkney, traditional practices seem to have continued without obvious disruption until after 3000.

CHAPTER FOUR

Temples of the earth and sky 3000 to 2500 BC

Temples

During this period, at different times in different places, people ceased to bury their dead in chambered tombs. The first large circular ceremonial earthworks were built within a generation or so of 3000. Tall timber and stone rings were set up; lower stone rings had been built much earlier, at least in Argyll and north-east Scotland, but whatever idea they represented was transmuted into a more impressive form. Ritual became less centred round the land and more on the movements of the sun and moon.

This period of overlap around 3000, when both tombs and stone rings were important, was a time of people whose authority was focused around rituals related to both the earth and sky. The new ideas swept through much of Britain. In some areas of Scotland there is little sign that they were practised; in Shetland and the north-east, as before and after this date, new versions of old practices dominated rituals and, probably, everyday life (35).

Shetland

The earliest dated evidence for burial in Shetland comes from a rough small cairn, close to House 1 of the settlement at Scord of Brouster and 75m (250ft) from where House 2 had been built in the previous period, and from an inhumation in a massive burial cist at Sumburgh. Perhaps they are a sign that the heel-shaped tombs so characteristic of Shetland, none of which have been dated, were going out of use.

Farming at Scord of Brouster in Shetland flourished and the largest building, House 1, was constructed around the middle of this period. As with House 2 in the previous period, the first phase of occupation left no surviving walls; its nature is obscure. It was succeeded by an oval house defined by an earth and rubble bank with an internal wall-face; like many oval Shetland houses it had hardly any external face (36). Stones set near the wall defined six shallow, wide recesses, and in the central space there was a spread of hearths. The pottery from the house consisted of plain bowls. The dates for this and the next phase of building suggest the house was occupied for about five hundred years, or twenty generations, with no structural modification.

Round it was an area of infields in which barley will have been cultivated (37). The field walls of the earlier period continued in use and stones cleared from the fields were dumped against them. At some much later date, after peat had covered the ground and perhaps after the house had gone out of use, a massive kerb was added to the burial cairn near House 1.

35 *Map of sites radiocarbon dated to between 3000 and 2500.*

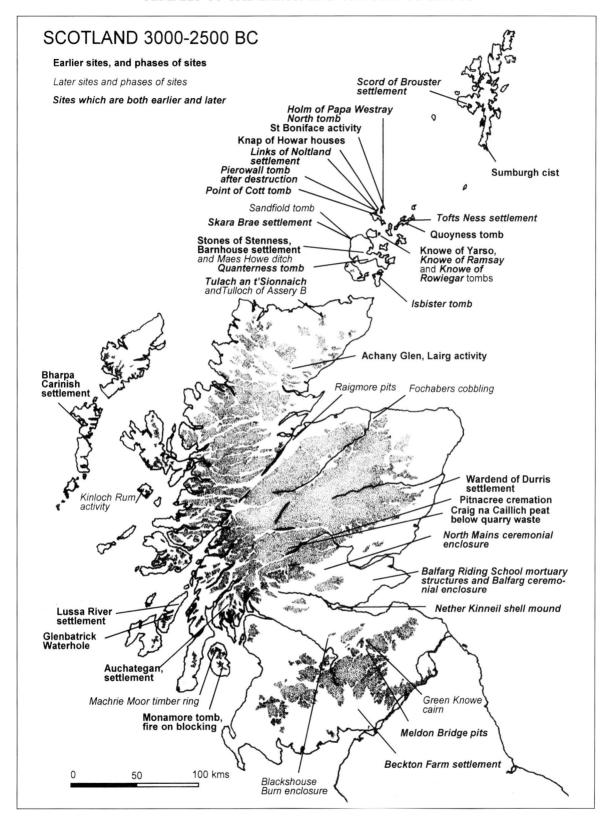

SCOTLAND 3000-2500 BC

Earlier sites, and phases of sites

Later sites and phases of sites

Sites which are both earlier and later

Scord of Brouster
settlement

Holm of Papa Westray
North tomb
St Boniface activity
Knap of Howar houses
Links of Noltland
settlement
Pierowall tomb
after destruction
Point of Cott tomb

Sandfield tomb

Skara Brae settlement

Stones of Stenness,
Barnhouse settlement
and Maes Howe ditch
Quanterness tomb

Tulach an t'Sionnaich
andTulloch of Assery B

Sumburgh cist

Tofts Ness settlement

Quoyness tomb

Knowe of Yarso,
Knowe of Ramsay
and **Knowe of**
Rowiegar tombs

Isbister tomb

Achany Glen, Lairg activity

Raigmore pits   *Fochabers cobbling*

Bharpa
Carinish
settlement

Kinloch Rum
activity

Wardend of Durris
settlement
Pitnacree cremation
Craig na Caillich peat
below quarry waste

North Mains ceremonial
enclosure

Balfarg Riding School mortuary
structures and Balfarg ceremo-
nial enclosure

Lussa River
settlement

Glenbatrick
Waterhole

Nether Kinneil shell mound

Auchategan,
settlement

Machrie Moor timber ring

Monamore tomb,
fire on blocking

Green Knowe
cairn

Meldon Bridge pits

Beckton Farm settlement

0   50   100 kms

Blackshouse
Burn enclosure

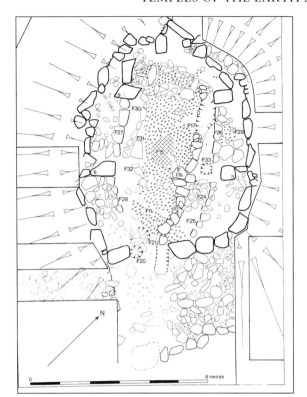

36 *The interior of House 1 at Scord of Brouster, in Shetland, measured 7 by 5.4m (23 by 18ft). The plan shows part of what was discovered during excavation. The inner wall-face was comparatively well built but the outer wall-face was very weak; perhaps it was originally made of turf, or perhaps a pitched roof sloped down over it almost to the ground, or it may simply have been robbed for building stone. The spaces created along the inner wall by projecting blocks seem to be too small for sleeping in, so perhaps the house had a special daytime purpose.*

37 *The same house at Scord of Brouster in Shetland as was shown in the previous illustration, but here reconstructed in this artist's impression. The cairn nearest to the house in this view was used for burials. The other cairns may simply represent clearance of the stony ground. The cultivated patches may not have been as neat as shown here.*

Orkney

In Orkney, deposition of human bones continued in at least two of the great tombs with shallow graceful bowls, Isbister and Point of Cott, until about the middle of this period. Rubble filled the chamber at Isbister shortly afterwards; a burial set in the rubble suggests the tomb was still remembered. Occupation continued at Knap of Howar after 3000, although perhaps not for long. The people who lived there may have buried their dead at Holm of Papa Westray North, the inner compartment of which, at least, was sealed up around 3000. Around 2500, the whole chamber and the passage were purposefully filled with earth and stones, judging by a date from a sheep bone. We have dates for red-deer bones in three other chambered tombs of a similar kind, with the same kind of pottery: Knowe of Yarso, the Knowe of Ramsay and the Knowe of Rowiegar, all on Rousay; but their excavations were not recorded to modern standards and the bones used for dating may have been deposited by feral dogs at a time when the tombs were not in use. Be that as it may, during the later half of this period most of the dates from the great and little tombs of Orkney come from animal bones. At Pierowall, described below, domestic structures had been built on a rough platform made from stones robbed from the cairn. It seems likely that most tombs were no longer commonly used for disposal of the dead after 2500.

There are at least fifteen chambered tombs on Rousay, even though the island is only 50sq km (20sq miles) in area. They seem to dominate cultivable areas, and although some cairns seem to overlook the same areas as their nearest neighbours, they may have been built to assert or consolidate land rights. The lack of pottery and human bones in some of them may reflect transfer of bones and ancestral artefacts to safer places, as different communities struggled for supremacy. Perhaps the Rousay tombs show us that there was a large element of ritual assertiveness, given expression in stone and

earth, which may usually have been an adequate substitute for violence.

Large chambered cairns in which grooved ware was deposited with the human remains had by now been built on several of the islands of the Orkney archipelago. Quoyness, on Sanday, was a complex round cairn. It had internal ring-walls which may mean that at least during its building it looked like a set of low solid towers of reducing width one on top of the other, but perhaps the walls were there just to give internal stability, and stones were later piled against the walls to produce a domed shape. At this period farming continued at Tofts Ness, also on Sanday. The excavated middens contained burnt turf, abundant animal bones and the articulated skeleton of a bull. The buildings lie mostly under a large mound beyond the excavated areas. A settlement at Pool, on Sanday, with several successive houses similar to those at Barnhouse, and deep middens with grooved ware, was probably occupied throughout most if not all of this period, although no suitable material was retrieved for radiocarbon dating.

At Pierowall on Westray, severe damage occurred to a chambered cairn at some time during the ten generations after 3000, judging by radiocarbon dates associable with the collapse of its revetment walls. It had been built by people who made grooved ware. Partial excavation of the edge of the cairn (because it seemed likely to collapse into a quarry) followed the discovery of extraordinarily fine carved stones (38) with similar decoration to that found on some grooved-ware pottery. Clearly this tomb had high prestige.

A settlement with grooved ware nearby, at Links of Noltland, seems to have been well established at this period. The excavations under the sand there revealed fields separated by walls, and one curious structure consisting of passages and a cell at a spot called Grobust. It was not, it seems, like any of the Neolithic houses or tombs which have been discovered in Orkney. The excavator has suggested that it

38 *Part of this fine carved stone was found during quarrying, and part during archaeological excavation, at Pierowall, on Westray in Orkney. It is 1.34m (4½ft) long. It was probably a lintel in the chambered cairn.*

served some ritual function. The extensive fields suggest that there are more structures, perhaps more like the houses at Barnhouse, waiting to be discovered.

Barnhouse, as described in Chapter 3, started off several generations before 3000 as a settlement of small houses like (but earlier than) those of the first period at Skara Brae. It seems

to have had one important double-sized house. At least one of the buildings (Structure 5) was demolished and rebuilt on the same spot as many as five times. Now, on the edge of the settlement closest to the henge and stone circle at Stenness an extraordinarily large structure was built, like an overgrown house on a circular platform surrounded by a wall (**colour plate 3**). Its elaborate entrance included a passage about 5m (16ft) long with a hearth at its threshold. Inside it had a central hearth and a dresser against its rear wall. In plan, house and platform were very like the ground-plan of the great chambered tomb of Maes Howe, but where the passage of Maes Howe points at midwinter sunset, the entrance of Structure 8 pointed to midsummer sunrise. It would be hard to imagine a more intuitively attractive symbolism.

Maes Howe is the finest chambered tomb in Britain. It sits on a clay platform and is surrounded by a broad circular ditch (**39** and see **colour plate 1**). Like Quoyness, the mound has internal walls, which at Maes Howe were certainly built to stabilize the mound rather than to be seen once it was completed. The large square central chamber was beautifully built of sandstone slabs, with three equally carefully constructed side cells entered at waist height. The chamber was reached by a long passage which was designed so it could be blocked up by a large stone, probably from inside, as if to hide what happened in the chamber, rather than from outside, for the door-checks against which it could be pushed were just to the outward side of the niche which housed the blocking stone when it was not in use.

The chamber did not have any pottery in it when it was excavated in 1861; but it is convincingly like other chambered tombs which contained grooved ware, and on one of the great buttresses which form the corners of the chamber is a carving exactly like one of those at the grooved-ware settlement of Skara Brae. So almost certainly the tomb was built by people like those who lived nearby at Barnhouse and carried out ceremonies at the Stones of Stenness.

1 *The burial chamber in the huge mound at Maes Howe, in Orkney, measures 4.7m (16ft) square; and was originally some 4.5m (15ft) high. It is reached through a passage 16m (53ft) long, which is aligned fairly close to midwinter sunset. Inset is a detail of a design carved on one of the great buttresses, which is similar to carvings found at the Skara Brae settlement (**colour plates 5** and **6**).*

2 *The larger house at Knap of Howar, on Papa Westray in Orkney, was about 9.6m (32ft) long internally and contained two rooms. The smaller one, shown here, was about 7.5m (25ft) long internally and had three rooms. They date to between 5500 and 5000 years ago.*

3 *Barnhouse Structure 8 (below and opposite), in Orkney, included a platform of yellow clay 21–23m (about 70–75ft) across, surrounded by a stone wall over 1m (3ft) thick. On the platform was a house or hall. Its walls were 3m (10ft) thick. The room inside them was 10.7m (over 35ft) long and 7.6m (25ft) wide.*

4 There were originally 11 or 12 tall
stones in the 31.2m (102ft) diameter
circle at Stenness, in Orkney. They
stood inside a 2.3m (8ft) deep ditch
with an external bank. The entrance
was due north of the centre of the
circle, where there was a large stone
hearth. Between the entrance and the
central hearth were several stone and
timber settings.

5 Most of the visible houses at Skara
Brae in Orkney are on much the same
sites as earlier ones. These sites were
used several times as houses were
rebuilt. The latest houses were larger
than the earliest ones and had box
beds built of large sandstone slabs
sticking out from the walls.

6 Ritual objects from Skara Brae include
carved stone balls and more complex
shapes. Fine objects like these may
have been symbols of power.

7 The ring of tall stones and the 4m (13ft) tall central monolith at Calanais in the Western Isles were set up on top of old cultivation ridges. The ring is about 10m (33ft) across; and is not a true circle, for its eastern side turns slightly inward. The axis of symmetry points east. A row of standing stones runs south from the ring at a right-angle to this axis and was perhaps set up at the same time as the ring. Other rows run roughly east and west, and an avenue of stones runs slightly east of north.

8 The two tall stone circles on Machrie Moor on Arran, in western Scotland, probably date to the centuries around 3000. They are part of a complex of six rings of stone and also timber rings in an area which was a centre for rituals from well before 3500.

9 *Easter Aquhorthies is one of the many 'recumbent stone' circles of north-east Scotland. They are called recumbent stone circles because, between two of their tallest standing stones, they include a huge stone lying on its side.*

10 *The hoard from Migdale, in northern Scotland, dates to the centuries around 2000. It contained many bronze objects: two narrow-butted flat axes, six simple rings and two flat, ridged rings (all big enough to fit a slim wrist), little tubes of sheet metal, a basket-shaped ear-ring, conical bead covers and a small highly decorated piece of sheet metal. In addition, there were at least five conical jet or shale buttons.*

11 Inside a low earthen wall which defined the house at Tormore, on Arran in western Scotland, was a wattle lining. The roof was supported by a ring of posts. The dark patches inside the wall are caused by charcoal, part of the evidence that the house was burnt down. Fragments of beaker pottery, reflecting both insular and continental traditions, were found inside it.

12 This artist's impression shows a bronzesmith at work in one house of a settlement at Jarlshof in Shetland. Weapons, tools and ornaments were made there.

The passage points south-west to where the sun sets on the days around the shortest day of the year. The blocking stone in the passage is slightly less tall than the passage and when in place it allowed the setting sun to shine through a horizontal slit at that time of the year, creating a dramatic bar of light on the back wall of the chamber.

In 1991, excavations at Maes Howe showed that the mound overlies an earlier monument, although not enough of it has been revealed to show what purpose it served. A stone drain which ran northward from the mound to the ditch may belong to this earlier building period or, given the meticulous care with which the rest of the monument was built, it may have been designed to drain water from the mound. Thus even this, one of the best-known monuments in Scotland, archaeologically excavated four times, still conceals important secrets

The earthwork at Stenness is one of the earliest three examples of a ceremonial enclosure of the kind archaeologists call henges. They are, typically, roughly circular and surrounded by a ditch with an external bank. Inside the ditch at

39 *Maes Howe, in Orkney, contains the finest chamber of any tomb in north-west Europe (see* **colour plate** *1). Its mound averages over 35m (115ft) across and it is over 7m (23ft) tall now. Originally it was about 1m taller. It sits on a partially artificial platform surrounded by a broad, shallow ditch. Excavation has shown that the visible mound and chamber were not the first monument here, but the form and purpose of its predecessors is as yet unclear.*

Stenness was a ring of tall stones; they would have been difficult to erect once the ditch was dug and seem most likely to be of the same date (**colour plate 4**). Animal bone in the base of the ditch near the northern entrance, and a cremation in the hearth at the centre of the ring, are dated to this period. A line of timber and stone settings stretching northward from this central hearth is very similar to the combination of hearth and entrance passageway inside the overgrown house at Barnhouse. They are so similar to each other, and the radiocarbon dates are so close to each other, that they must have served much the same purpose. In the same way, although less strongly, Maes Howe and the overgrown house at Barnhouse are similar to each other and of roughly the same period. Thus in the heart of Orkney there was a concentration of highly connected sites built by people who used grooved ware: a very fine settlement with one important house, a henge with a superb stone ring in it and the best chambered tomb in Britain. This expression of power, combining the old with the new, suggests chieftains had taken over the old institutions.

Also occupied in this period was the most famous Neolithic settlement in Britain, the small village of stone-built houses at Skara Brae, on the west coast of Orkney. Most of the buildings visible today belong to the second half of this period, but some belonging to the earlier half can still be seen. These earlier houses were free-standing like those at Barnhouse, and like many of the houses at Barnhouse, the earlier houses at Skara Brae have beds recessed into the walls (**40**).

Although the settlement at Barnhouse seems to have been abandoned by about the middle of this period, the village at Skara Brae continued to flourish. The houses were different in style from those of the first period, although their basic components (beds to either side, central hearth and dresser at the back) remained the same (**colour plate 5**). The floor-areas were twice as great, and the beds, instead of being built into the walls, were in the living-space and

40 *The first settlement at Skara Brae, in Orkney, is largely covered by later houses, and its full extent is not known. The earliest visible houses had a central hearth, box beds built into the side walls, and a stone dresser against the back wall.*

bounded by long slabs set on edge. The difference in house styles was the cumulative effect of many changes spread over generations; individual houses were built and rebuilt or demolished to make way for new structures throughout occupation of the settlement.

The stone walls of the houses were set into midden consisting mostly of shells, with animal bones, pottery and other rubbish. Furniture was made of stone, including dressers used, perhaps, for the display of cult objects (**colour plate 6**). One building, alas undated, was of a very different plan. It was more oval in shape than the normal houses (indeed, it looks like contemporary houses in Shetland). It had a porch and stood isolated beyond an open space at the south-west end of the settlement. It has been interpreted as a workshop since it contained abundant remains of flintworking. As at Barnhouse, ritual and domestic activity were so entwined that they cannot be distinguished. Lightly scratched triangles and other shapes, similar to those found at Maes Howe, were found close to doors and to divisions in the passages connecting the houses.

Most of the houses seem to have been emptied of their contents before the settlement was abandoned. House 7, however, was different. Its floor and the beds were covered in bits of bone, pottery, tools and ornaments. A complete bull's skull lay on one bed. There was a bone dish full of red pigment on the floor, and a cache of beads and pendants was found in a cell at the back of the room. Two women had been buried in the room, one in a stone cist, and although it is not clear from the original excavation account whether the graves were earlier than the house or inserted through the floor during its use, it does seem that this was a special place. It may even have continued in use after the rest of the settlement was abandoned.

Not far from Skara Brae, at Sandfield, the first burial occurred in a remarkable rock-cut tomb. Perhaps it and the massive cist at Sumburgh on Shetland mark a time of change, when chambered tombs went out of use. Both burial places lacked a cairn, and if the cairns of chambered tombs had served as symbols of the power of the local community they suggest that such symbols were no longer appropriate. This fits well with the suggestion that power was centralized at around 3000.

The north

South of Orkney and north of Dornoch there are no known grooved-ware centres, although a few objects found in tombs seem quite like those found on grooved-ware sites. Perhaps they represent gifts rather than the nearby presence of settlements or ceremonial enclosures. However, it seems that here, too, the chambered tombs were abandoned during this period. Only animal bones was put in Tulach an t'Sionnaich and Tulloch of Assery B, although paving was laid over the deer bones at the latter site and it does seem likely it remained in some sort of use. Perhaps ceremonials other than those to do with disposal of the dead had always taken place at tombs, and these continued in a new form involving burial of animal bones. There is a little evidence for agriculture in Achany Glen, south of Lairg, but perhaps in parallel with disuse of the chambered cairns the settlement focus in this area had moved away from the areas which have been excavated.

At Raigmore, grooved-ware sherds with flints and burnt bone were deposited in a pit during the ten generations before 2500, and an unaccompanied cremation was placed in another. The building at Raigmore is very like the structures at Balfarg Riding School discussed below, except that it had a hearth and it did not have complicated internal post structures. It may be the remains of a house with rounded corners and straight sides (**41**).

The east

At much the same time as the henge at Stenness, two house-like structures were built at Balfarg Riding School, enclosing platforms on which bodies were exposed, and a roughly circular ditched enclosure was dug round the later of them (**42**). Grooved ware was found in the holes in which the posts had stood and was incorporated in a low mound covering the later of the two structures. Each of them was about 18m (60ft) long by half as wide, straight

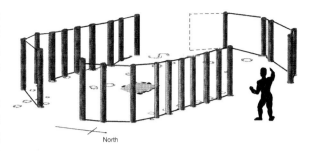

North

41 *At least two successive structures were built of posts at Raigmore, near Inverness in northern Scotland. The central hearth has suggested to some that it was a house; but as the reconstruction diagram shows, it is difficult to see how it could have been roofed. In the diagram, posts have been assigned to post-holes in a way which to the modern eye appears to make sense. The horizontal lines are meant to suggest the tops and bottoms of wattle panels. Perhaps the enclosure hid rituals surrounding the cremation of human bones from the people excluded from the ceremonies.*

42 *This artist's impression of one of the structures at Balfarg Riding School, in eastern Scotland, illustrates how it probably consisted of two main elements: a curtain-wall of wicker panels supported by posts, and pairs of posts inside supporting platforms for the exposure of dead bodies. The evidence here was of a higher quality than at Raigmore (see **41**) and allows a more confident interpretation.*

sided with rounded corners, built of posts set at about 1.25m (4ft) intervals. It seems quite likely that they were closely related in shape to contemporary and earlier houses, perhaps including the loosely dated structure at Raigmore, reflecting the tradition of round-cornered straight-sided houses found in several parts of Scotland in the period from 4000 to 3000. However, careful analysis of the sizes and spacing of the many post-holes inside them suggests that they were not roofed over but surrounded platforms used for exposing dead bodies. If so, they represent another variant on the constant theme of the Neolithic period, special places for disposal of the dead.

Round the later of the two structures was a roughly circular enclosure about 40m (130ft) across. It was defined by a ditch about 3m (10ft) wide and 1m (3ft) deep, with perhaps a slight bank. Grooved-ware pottery had been deposited in it, and much charcoal with remains of sloe berries, crab-apple, hazel and what may have been the pod of a legume, giving another insight into the varied diet available at this time, even though these particular remains may be the remains of some ritual rather than everyday food.

One of the grooved-ware potsherds at Balfarg Riding School had carbonized encrustations containing henbane, a potent hallucinogenic. It would be foolish to suppose all grooved ware in all circumstances was used for ceremonies including drug-induced hazes, but we can perhaps suppose we have a partial explanation for the burial of purposefully smashed pots in this and earlier periods. Hallucinogens seem to have been used throughout Europe during the Neolithic period and judging by ethnographic parallels could have played a part in rituals.

The circular enclosure at Balfarg Riding School seems, along with Stenness, to be one of the three earliest henges known (the word henge was first used archaeologically to describe the ditched enclosure around Stonehenge, and large ceremonial enclosures defined by ditches with external banks). So the origin of henges may have been either in rituals associated with formal disposal of remains of the dead or in rituals replacing formal disposal. Henges are important because they appear to mark a change in society in the centuries around 3000. Where chambered tombs may represent centres for ritual and disposal of the dead for small communities, large henges seem to be meeting-places for ceremonies involving the communities of much larger areas. Indeed, some of the southern English examples, like Avebury, are immense works; their construction required very large workforces. It is generally thought that they mark significant changes in society, including centralization of power into a few hands. Most (but not all) seem to have been used by people who also used grooved ware.

A few generations after the henge had been built at Balfarg Riding School, a much larger one was constructed nearby at Balfarg. It had an entrance at the west, and it seems also to have had an entrance to the south (43). Inside it there were probably several timber circles, of which that built of the largest timbers consisted of 16 posts. The timbers in the eastern part of this ring were much shorter than those to the west, where two posts, set just outside the ring, probably defined an entrance. Intriguingly, it did not line up exactly with the entrance to the earthwork. There may have been two other wicker or wattle ring-fences of greater diameters. Subsequently, probably, two stone circles were built inside the earthwork. The innermost stone circle may have been composed of about 12 stones and the other of 24 stones. The pottery associated with early use of the enclosure was grooved ware. However, more or less central to the earthwork (but not central to the timber rings) was a later burial of a young adult with a handled beaker (see Chapter 5 for a description of beakers).

At much the same time as the henge at Balfarg, to within a generation or so, another henge was built at North Mains in Perthshire.

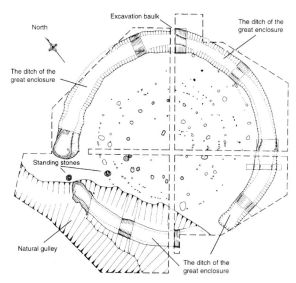

43 *The plan shows excavation of the large ritual enclosure at Balfarg, in eastern Scotland. Sections have been cut across the ditch, which is the main circular feature. It enclosed an area about 65m (215ft) across. At the bottom of the picture a large natural gully is shown, with the ditch running through it between two causeways. Baulks of earth, left as a record of soil depths, form a cross shape, here outlined with dashed lines, as is the edge of the huge excavation area.*

Evidence survived for several timber circles in the area enclosed by the ditch. The one with the largest post-holes was built of 16 massive timbers and was about 38m (125ft) across. The timbers in the western part of this ring were taller than those on the eastern side. At least one stone circle was built in the area inside the ditch, consisting of about 12 stones, one of which stands today about 1.6m (5ft 4in) tall. Nearby, another similar standing stone also survives, set on the north-western entrance causeway. There may have been another ring of 24 stones, built just inside the inner lip of the ditch.

Outside the ditch was a bank (its presence was deduced from the way the ditch filled up, and it is not shown on this plan). The relationship between ditch and bank was thus the opposite of that seen in defensive earthworks.

As with so many of the important sites of this period, there had been earlier burials and other activities near the site. Now 24 large timber posts were set up to form a ring, flattened on its north side. A broad, flat-bottomed ditch, with a massive external bank, was dug round them. There were two entrances, one in the eastern half and the other opposite it (**44**). A circle of timber posts, smaller in diameter than the main one, and set off-centre, may have been earlier than the main circle and the earthwork.

The similarities between Balfarg and North Mains are obvious; but so are their differences. The earthwork at Balfarg enclosed four or five times the area of that at North Mains. North Mains seems to have had taller posts, and the variable depths of the post-holes suggest that the posts stood to the same height. In contrast, the Balfarg posts rose in height from east to west to meet a special entrance arrangement. It seems most likely that the posts preceded the earthwork at North Mains (if only by a few days) whereas there is just a suggestion that the posts at Balfarg were put up after the earthwork had been completed.

Since there is no uniformity in detail between these two monuments it is risky to try to interpret the more damaged monument, Balfarg, by other sites which may be just as different in their particulars. Nevertheless, the timber and stone rings at Machrie Moor (described below in this chapter) provide some ideas, since their stratigraphy was so much clearer. There, timber and subsequently stone circles were built over a very long period, with an intervening period of agriculture. The complexities at Balfarg probably represent a similarly long history.

That length of history pales into insignificance when it is compared to the period over which shells were thrown on to the massive midden at Nether Kinneil, from before 3250 to nearly 2000 and in every period between.

The south

Dates from pits under a cairn at Harehope near Eddleston in Peebleshire suggest the site was used for disposal of the dead before 2500

44 *This air photograph shows the ceremonial enclosure at North Mains, in eastern Scotland, before excavation. Its ditch, with its two entrance causeways, shows up clearly to the right of the small wood. Post-holes are visible inside it. In them, 24 large timber posts were set up, forming a ring about 25 by 27m (82 by 89ft) across, flattened on its north side. The posts stood 5–7m (16–23ft) tall. The massive earthwork built round them consisted of a bank, perhaps 9m (30ft) wide and 2m (7ft) tall, outside the broad, flat-bottomed ditch visible on the photograph, which was generally about 7m (23ft) across and 2–3m (7–10ft) deep, and enclosed an area about 30m (100ft) across.*

(45). They came from small roundwood charcoal among a scatter of cremated bone and potsherds from a disturbed pit, and from a pit containing oak charcoal. The pot seems to have some of the characteristics of grooved ware and some of beakers, which will be described in Chapter 5. Harehope was interpreted by its excavator as a low cairn robbed of its stones, but the rings of small stones thought to represent kerbs may instead have been free-standing. Not many kilometres further south down a narrow river valley is Meldon Bridge, where pottery with impressed decoration reflecting a different tradition was buried in a pit in the centuries before 2500.

Pits were dug at the settlement at Beckton near Lockerbie throughout this period, one of them with flints in it and two others with grooved ware. Yet another contained coarse pottery possibly burnt where it was found. There

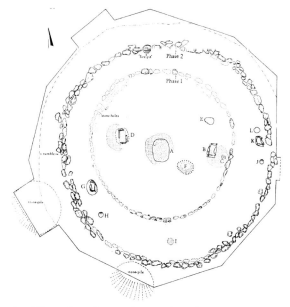

45 *This plan shows the results of excavation of the cairn at Harehope, in south-eastern Scotland, where an area nearly 20m (65ft) across was used for burials for several centuries. It is difficult to reconstruct its appearance at any given time, but at some stage a kerb of small stones enclosed a low cairn or open area about 10.5m (34ft) across (the inner ring here). Between 2500 and 2000 a large central pit was dug for a burial with jet beads (see Chapter 5, and **54**). Subsequently there were more burials, and the whole area was eventually surrounded by a kerb of larger stones (the outer ring here) which may have retained a low cairn.*

are records of a large enclosure with grooved ware and other pottery nearby, destroyed during road building, and it seems quite likely that Beckton was a settlement forming part of a complex of monuments with a general similarity to the complexes at Barnhouse, Balfarg, Machrie Moor (where contemporary settlement has still to be identified) and elsewhere.

The west

Seemingly late in this period a large enclosure was built at Blackshouse Burn in Lanarkshire. It is not readily comparable with the enclosures at Balfarg and North Mains described above. Its bank was built of timber, earth and stones enclosing a large somewhat irregular area, but

no ditch either inside or outside. Little is known about the interior of the enclosure, apart from a suggestion of small low mounds. Although it undoubtedly was a regional or local centre it is difficult to know whether to compare it with the structure built at Meldon Bridge around 2500 (discussed in Chapter 5) or with the more formal round enclosures already discussed.

At Machrie Moor, around 3000, an almost perfect circle of about fifty timbers was built. Inside the circle was a horseshoe-shaped timber setting of very large posts, open to the north-west (**46**). Grooved ware from one pot was found both in the construction levels of the circle and in the destruction levels of the horseshoe, which may thus be earlier than 3000. The posts of the horseshoe were so large they may have survived (as may the circle, since some of its posts were replaced) for some fifteen to twenty-five generations, after which a wide ring of slight and closely spaced fence posts (perhaps supporting a wicker or wattle fence) was erected round the area. Perhaps the fence excluded some of the community from rituals; or it may simply have served to define a sacred area. Another timber circle was built less than 20m (67ft) away at some time between 3000 and 2500. It consisted of ten posts in a circle of much the same size as that around the horseshoe; and it may have been a response to growing divisions in society with different groups focusing their ceremonies on different structures.

The story of this period is not just about ceremonial sites. One of two or more small houses at Auchategan on Bute has been dated to the generations after 3000. The shape of the house was defined by a roughly circular area scraped out of the soft bedrock, and stake-holes showed that it was built in part of light wooden poles (**47**). A succession of hearths suggested that occupation lasted for many years, and perhaps the reason why the house-plan was so difficult to trace was that the structures were built largely of turf, or the houses had been robbed to build later structures, although one early

46 *The photograph includes two of the (later) stone circles at Machrie Moor on Arran, in western Scotland, during excavation. Fig. 56 shows their complete circuits. The excavation revealed timber circles dating to just after 3000. In the foreground are some of the holes dug for a horseshoe-shaped setting, measuring about 5 by 3m (16 by 10ft), built of very tall, massive posts. A ramp can be seen leading down into one of the holes. Other pits and post-holes are visible nearby. Between the standing stones can be seen the post-holes of the main timber ring of fifty 2.5m (8ft) tall timbers. It was about 14.5m (48ft) in diameter. It is extraordinary, given the many centuries which separated them, that the stone circle was built on exactly the same circuit as the timber ring. In the background is the other excavated stone circle, which had also been preceded by a timber ring.*

house was partially outlined with stones. The abundant pottery consisted of round-bottomed bowls, of a kind rarely found in the burial chambers of tombs of the region, like Monamore on the nearby island of Arran and Port Charlotte on Islay, but it has a general similarity to that found immediately under the topmost layer of material blocking the forecourt of the chambered cairn at Monamore at much the same date. It seems, on this admittedly slender evidence, that chambered tombs went out of use in Argyll at about the same time as in the north, strengthening the impression that change swept through the whole of Scotland.

The Western Isles

Over in the Western Isles, the settlement at Bharpa Carinish probably ended. As described in Chapter 3, since the one thing lacking was convincing wall lines, the excavator's suggestion that the houses were probably built of turf may be correct; robbing is an alternative explanation. Turf was probably an important building material at all periods of Scotland's prehistory and history prior to modern times, which might explain why some other western Scottish settlement sites have not produced clear house-plans.

Centres of power

Society changed around 3000. Previously the land was covered by small groups of people with local allegiances. Now centres for widespread groups became more important. The old loose networks of connections between people linked by kinship, exchange of goods and support in hard times was partially replaced by a more sophisticated system. The heart of Orkney demonstrates all the components one might expect if some powerful idea had concentrated resources from a large area in one place. It had a settlement much larger than those of earlier periods. It had a dramatic ceremonial site. It had an extraordinary tomb. The changes are associated with the spread of grooved ware; and it and the henges, circular ceremonial enclosures like those at Stenness and at Balfarg Riding School, seem to be earlier than elsewhere in Britain.

The stone ring at Calanais was perhaps part of an equivalent complex serving the northern part of the Western Isles (**colour plate 7**). Although undated, the ring of tall stones was probably built around this time on top of abandoned cultivation ridges; excavation has shown that the tiny chambered tomb in the eastern half of the ring of stones at Calanais is definitely later than the ring of stones; yet it is unlikely to have been built much after 3000. Further, although there are no radiocarbon dates from the site itself, there is a set of dates from a nearby pollen column which suggests considerable human activity in the area at about 3000. Inside the ring, under the tomb, excavation has revealed part of a small structure associated with grooved ware, so it seems likely that Calanais was used by people with links to the great ritual centres with grooved ware.

Similarly tall stone circles at Machrie Moor may have been put up in the same period, and the many stone and timber rings suggest it was the regional centre for Arran and perhaps nearby parts of the mainland (**colour plate 8**). However, radiocarbon dating shows that the other stone circles at Machrie Moor, made of massive but stubby stones, were demonstrably built much later. By 2500, however, there are signs that the rituals of different parts of society had become divided, for at Machrie and

47 *The photograph shows the valley-side setting of the houses at Auchategan, Argyll, in western Scotland. The excavation trench is visible near the bottom left of the photo, just beyond the dramatic scars of forestry ploughing. The photograph illustrates the point that ancient sites cannot be understood except in the context of their contemporary landscapes. The siting of the settlement well above the valley floor is of considerable interest. Perhaps the valley soils were too poorly drained for either agriculture or settlement until modern times. The remains of this period were found under later structures and little remained to define their shape. Their walls may have been built largely of turf lined with wattle or wicker panels supported on light poles.*

possibly at Calanais more than one structure had been built. They still clustered quite near one another, but this change foreshadowed a time when each small group of communities would have its own ritual centre.

In this period, too, there is evidence for alignment of major structures on astronomical events, for the passage at Maes Howe points at sunset on the days around midwinter. There is, then, just a suggestion that a phenomenon which appeared throughout Britain, signs of a religion or at least a set of beliefs encapsulating astronomical phenomena like the movements of the sun and the moon, and great ceremonial centres with grooved ware deposited in them, originated in Scotland. Its development started several generations before 3000 and it reached a peak in Scotland between 3000 and 2750. It is possible that the new set of ideas spread fast because it was attractive to incipient chieftain-ships elsewhere, helping them concentrate power in their own hands. It is even conceiv-able that people took the new practices south with them. That said, there were large parts of Scotland where the new ideas caught on hardly at all: Shetland, north, north-east and south-east Scotland seem, on present evidence, to have been largely immune.

Prehistoric astronomy

There was a consistent preference for pointing earthen long cairns and barrows in a broadly easterly direction. The earliest dated seemingly precise astronomical orientation was at Temple Wood, perhaps as early as the period 3750 to 3500 but certainly before 3000. The passage at Maes Howe, probably built around 3000, points at the setting sun on the days around the shortest day of the year. Many other types of monument – particularly ceremonial and burial monuments – demonstrate consistent local preferences for general orientation, some types to the south-west and others in other directions.

Alexander Thom, among others, has made a case for more sophisticated alignments on more subtle astronomical phenomena such as the extreme northerly rising and setting of the moon, which occurs every 18.6 years. He has suggested that some alignments of stones point accurately at notches on the horizon where the sun, the moon or bright stars set at particularly significant times of the year.

Thom's theories are important. There is noth-ing surprising about his simpler propositions, because societies in a similar state of organiza-tion display great sophistication in their responses to the movements of the sun, moon and stars and weave them into their ways of life. However, many archaeologists are uneasy about his use of archaeological information, pointing to errors in surveys and to unjustified assump-tions about the accuracy with which it is possible to reconstruct the alignments. They also point out that, at sites with many stones, so many possible alignments can be identified that it is likely some would appear significant purely by chance. Thom's adherents suggest that if we required the same level of proof for any of our archaeological ideas as we demand for his there is nothing we can say about prehistory at all beyond a drab catalogue of pots and post-holes. Clive Ruggles, a reformed astrophysicist at Leicester University, has in my view shown that, although Thom may be right, his more sophisti-cated ideas cannot be *proved* to be right. In sum, while there can be no doubt at all that the prehistoric people of Scotland did align some of their monuments on astronomical events, we have not yet got the evidence to demonstrate exactly at what level of sophistication, or how commonly, astronomical beliefs were expressed in the temples and tombs. Similarly, we cannot tell what calendars, if any, were in use, nor when festivals were celebrated.

CHAPTER FIVE

Cults or conquerors
2500 to 2000 BC

There is little evidence for any significant change in climate between 2500 and 2000. The overall impression is that the settlements and ceremonial enclosures with grooved ware, which seemingly expressed a centralization of power within quite wide areas, were no longer being built anew (**48**). Indeed, grooved ware itself went out of use before 2250. At about the same time new styles of pot appear, some of them with continental origins. These latter pots are usually graceful with an S-shaped profile, simple rims and abundant decoration. Archaeologists call them beakers (**49**).

Beakers and burials

Until very recently beakers provided fertile ground for typological schemes, which were supposed to reflect chronology. Excavation reports faithfully estimated the place of each beaker in the schemes. The best-known are the Dutch Step System and David L. Clarke's system of exotic and insular beakers. The Dutch Step System was devised to describe changes in the form and decoration of beaker pottery in the Netherlands, based on the evidence from deeply stratified sites and associations with other artefacts, and also on radiocarbon dates. Its authors recommended that their methods be used elsewhere to devise local successions of beaker pottery types. Clarke's scheme was largely based on typology; that is to say, he divided up the known British beakers into

groups based on their shape and decoration and used the (very limited) evidence from stratigraphy and associations with other artefacts to define the chronological relationships between his groups. Then he examined continental dating schemes and postulated two main waves of influence from the continent of Europe, together with local developments, to explain and give approximate dates to changes in the shape and decoration of British beakers.

The main result of a dating programme organized by the British Museum is that neither scheme is supported in Britain by the radiocarbon dates. This may partly be due to the coarseness of radiocarbon dating. Probably, however, the underlying reason why typologies do not work for British beakers is that changes in pottery styles took place in different ways in different areas.

Beakers were present on the north-western fringes of the European mainland before they were made in Britain, and there were perfectly respectable predecessors for them there. Some British beakers are very like continental ones. Beakers which look similar to each other are found in widely separated parts of Britain, yet at the same time those in northern Britain tend to look more like each other than like beakers found in southern Britain.

What explanations can we attach to these facts? They should have a considerable significance for what beakers represent, and for an understanding of the strength of social

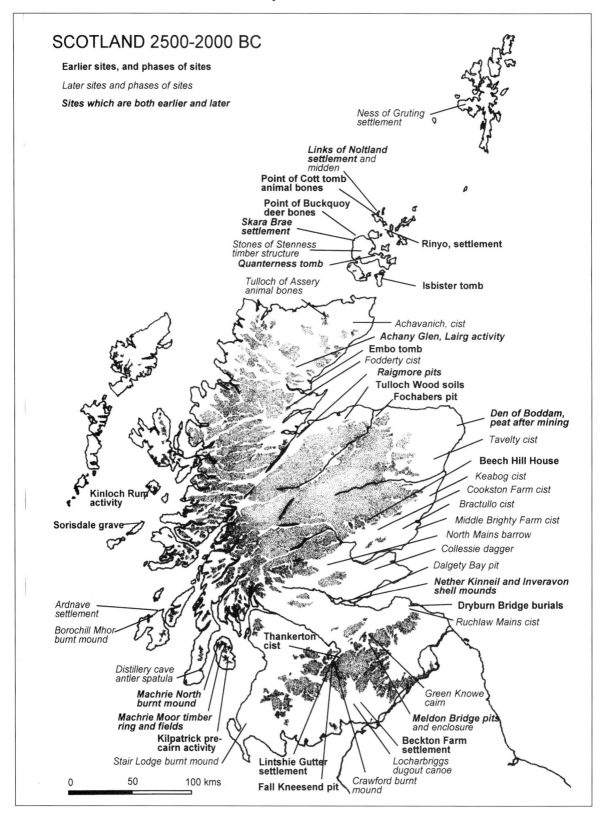

SCOTLAND 2500-2000 BC

Earlier sites, and phases of sites

Later sites and phases of sites

Sites which are both earlier and later

Ness of Gruting settlement

***Links of Noltland settlement** and midden*

Point of Cott tomb animal bones

Point of Buckquoy deer bones

Skara Brae settlement

Stones of Stenness timber structure

Quanterness tomb

Rinyo, settlement

Tulloch of Assery animal bones

Isbister tomb

Achavanich, cist

Achany Glen, Lairg activity

Embo tomb

Fodderty cist

Raigmore pits

Tulloch Wood soils

Fochabers pit

Den of Boddam, peat after mining

Tavelty cist

Beech Hill House

Keabog cist

Cookston Farm cist

Bractullo cist

Middle Brighty Farm cist

North Mains barrow

Collessie dagger

Dalgety Bay pit

Nether Kinneil and Inveravon shell mounds

Dryburn Bridge burials

Ruchlaw Mains cist

Kinloch Rum activity

Sorisdale grave

Ardnave settlement

Borochill Mhor burnt mound

Thankerton cist

Distillery cave antler spatula

Machrie North burnt mound

Machrie Moor timber ring and fields

Kilpatrick pre-cairn activity

Stair Lodge burnt mound

Green Knowe cairn

***Meldon Bridge pits** and enclosure*

Beckton Farm settlement

Locharbriggs dugout canoe

Lintshie Gutter settlement

Crawford burnt mound

Fall Kneesend pit

0   50   100 kms

48 *Map of sites radiocarbon dated to between 2500 and 2000.*

connections between different communities during this period. They should, too, be useful for an understanding of why and when the first Scottish beakers were made. We have the usual possibilities, ranging between introduction of a cult, fashion or religion through an exchange of ideas and gifts and, at another extreme, invasion.

Invasion is not a particularly useful concept in archaeology, because it is so difficult to prove even when we know it happened; although that should be no reason to dismiss the possibility of actual movement of groups of real live people when objects and structures found in one area are subsequently found in another. After all, once the written history of Scotland starts there are accounts of the Romans, the Scots, the Angles and the Norse, followed by Anglo-Normans, Flemings and a host of others. Each group arrived in different numbers, each from a different direction, some peacefully and others aggressively, over different lengths of time. Perhaps, then, groups of people using beakers did cross over the North Sea.

That said, history tells us too of exchanges of ideas, and the taking up of foreign fashions. It was suggested in the 1970s that we should compare the beaker phenomenon with the peyote cults of America. There the smoking of hallucinogenic peyote spread very rapidly north from Mexico to Canada in the decades after AD 1850, and took with it a package of things including rattles, a carved staff, a feather fan, a small drum and a crescent-shaped altar of clay or earth. This 'package' is rather different from what we see in the archaeological sites of Britain, although we may note in passing that of the peyote cult package all that would survive in the archaeological record in a British climate would be the small clay altar. In Britain the objects found with beakers include archers' gear, copper daggers and double-ended awls, and jet

and shale V-perforated buttons; a range of objects apparently different from those associated with the peyote cult not only in detail but also in general character. The analogy was intended, however, only to illustrate how a whole set of alien objects can be transmitted with some new, popular custom borrowed from afar.

I shall discuss the evidence with a particular emphasis on distinguishing between an invasion led by beaker-using chieftains (an idea very prevalent in British prehistory before the Second World War) and adoption of a religion, fashion or cult by indigenous communities through the exchange of gifts and ideas with neighbouring groups of people. The evidence is complex, particularly since it would be misleading to look at those sites with beakers in isolation from those without. I shall, as in previous chapters, consider the radiocarbon-dated evidence from north to south, to give a picture of what was happening throughout Scotland. We shall see the last gasps of the old order. Some sites will sway us towards ideas of beaker

49 *The Sorisdale beaker comes from Coll, a large island in western Scotland. It is one of the earliest dated beakers found in Britain. It accompanied a burial in a pit. This style of pottery was undoubtedly based on continental prototypes, but indigenous potting traditions remained important (see 52).*

chieftains. Others will indicate instead continuation of indigenous traditions in new forms. I shall summarize the evidence at the end.

Shetland

House 1, the largest house at Scord of Brouster, was slightly remodelled at the beginning of this period. Stones were placed across the open sides of the recesses which flanked the central area. Probably farming continued in the area without major interruption throughout this twenty-generation period.

Dates for a hoard of carbonized barley from the base of a wall of a house at Ness of Gruting, in what seems most likely to have been a foundation deposit, suggest the house was built around 2000. The house was of a type commonly found in Shetland, oval, with thick walls (50). It contained over six hundred stone implements including many stone ploughshares, and pottery which has been described as sharing Neolithic and beaker characteristics: more prosaically it might called a regional style of pottery. The house was part of a multi-period complex of fields and houses on the seaward side of a low hill separating it from the so-called temple at Stanydale.

Orkney

In Orkney, we have several dates for the final occupation at Skara Brae, suggesting it went out of use before 2250, while at Links of Noltland the structure at Grobust was carefully filled up with layers of midden. It may be that this almost ceremonial closing of the structure was similar to the purposeful filling in of chambered cairns. Nearby, the complete skeletons of red deer were found on top of a midden dating to the centuries immediately after 2500. Perhaps there is a prosaic explanation: the deer may have been invading crops and have been killed and skinned but not eaten. Perhaps the skeletons represent some sort of ritual slaughter. A later midden belong-

50 *The house at Ness of Gruting, Shetland, was dug about 1m (3ft) into the ground. This photograph shows it after excavation. The living-space was 10–11m (33–36ft) long by 4m (13ft) wide, including beds or benches along the side walls and a broad shelf at the back (far) end. As with many prehistoric Shetland houses the inner face of the wall was well built, but the outer face (not visible on this photograph) was much less well defined.*

ing in the ten generations before 2000 contained rather different evidence: a site in which several red deer had been butchered. There are a few sherds of beaker from this midden; and although beaker pottery is so far remarkable for its near absence from Orkney, it may be the hunters came from a group which lived nearby, rather than one which lived elsewhere and beached its boats to hunt on the island. There is also a date for red-deer bones from the point of Buckquoy, near to Birsay, another coastal site. A radiocarbon date from the grooved-ware settlement at Rinyo on Rousay suggests it was occupied around the middle of this period. It is curious that Rousay seems not to have any grooved-ware tombs. Perhaps Rinyo was built and occupied entirely at a time when tomb building was no longer fashionable.

The north

At Tulloch of Assery B, in Caithness, and at a few other tombs in this period, animal bones may reflect use of the old chambers as dens by carnivores. In Sutherland, there is evidence for agriculture in Achany Glen just south of Lairg throughout the period from 2500 to 2000. The ten-generation period between 2250 and 2000 seems also to have seen particularly intensive land use there. The evidence is somewhat difficult to interpret because, during this and later periods, intensive agriculture led to soil erosion on the valley slopes where the excavations were concentrated. Thus archaeological evidence would have been removed almost as fast as it was created. There, too, cremations were located during excavation of much younger buildings, under which they had been protected from at least some later prehistoric ploughing.

At Embo, in eastern Sutherland, many burials with beakers were placed in a chambered tomb. If there had been an incursion of people using beakers, they may have used a highly traditional type of burial place as part of a claim to the land. Alternatively, and perhaps more credibly, the pottery with the burials shows that an indigenous population adopted a fashion or cult involving the use of beakers. The evidence is thus fairly neutral.

Further south at Raigmore, near Inverness, two pits with grooved-ware pottery are dated to the earlier half of this period. Probably at some time before 2000 a rough circle of stubby stones (more a large kerb than a stone circle) had been set up here, for in the centuries around 2000 a food vessel was buried in a rough cist set against the kerb. Food vessels, although flat bottomed, share the decorative characteristics of some earlier types of pottery found in the south-east and east of Scotland. They seem to represent a reformulation of earlier potting traditions and they became common throughout Scotland before 2000.

The north-east

At Boghead, Fochabers, a pit with both plain and simply decorated beaker sherds belongs in this period while further east at Keabog, near Stonehaven, a middle-aged man with a

fractured skull was buried at some time during the centuries around 2000 in a stone cist with a beaker; close by, and not distinguishably different in date, was a cist containing a young man, also with a fractured skull, accompanied by a beaker and a flint knife. Here, perhaps, we have the sort of evidence which led people to think in terms of invasions: sturdy men who seem to have died through violence, buried with beakers.

The east

Down south in Perthshire, at Beech Hill House, soil found under a burial cairn may have been cultivated towards the beginning of this period. It contained sherds of grooved ware; but it may be that the date came from mixed charcoal, some contemporary with the grooved ware and some, perhaps, generations younger. There is also a date from oak charcoal in a burial cist with a cremation accompanied by a bone dagger pommel, a toggle and quartz sphere.

At North Mains, close to the ceremonial earthwork enclosure and timber rings, the building of a huge burial mound began, on top of a field, during the ten generations before 2000. The field was covered in narrow agricultural ridging, produced by spade or hoe cultivation. The ridges measured about 2m (6–7ft) from crest to crest and were designed to increase soil depth and warmth and improve drainage. Scanty pollen in the soil suggested that there was not much pasture in the area; rather there was heathland and scattered clumps of trees.

First a central pear-shaped area was defined by a fence built in straight-line segments; its northern half was built of much lighter stakes than in the south and west. In the east two lines of posts radiated away from the area, defining an entrance way. Light fences radiated in other directions from the central area, creating bays within which turves and subsoil were dumped to form a broad ring bank (**51**).

51 *At North Mains, in eastern Scotland, a fenced area 6.8–7.5m (22–25ft) across was surrounded by a broad bank. This artist's reconstruction drawing shows it before it was filled in to form a mound 40m (130ft) across and 5.5m (18ft) high. Clearly visible are the light fences which radiated from the open space through the temporary bank. Only half of the material used to build the mound came from the ditch at its base, which was up to 8.5m (28ft) wide by 2m (6–7ft) deep. The rest must have been scraped up from the ground around the mound.*

Perhaps burials were placed in the central area, though this cannot be proved. It did not stand open for long. The next stage was the building of the mound itself. The fence lines which defined the central area and the work areas were maintained nearly to the top of the mound – new fencing was erected as the mound grew upward. In the final stages of construction it was coated with turf and after a bonfire had been lit in a central hollow it was covered with boulders. At some stage a large cup-marked slab was incorporated in the topmost levels of the mound. Two burials with food vessels and eight cremations (most of them including the bones of more than one person) were set into the mound, most in small rough cists.

Was this, then, the burial place of a beaker chieftain, as might be expected if the idea of invasion were correct? Far from it. The pots associated with both the building of the mound and the burials in it were food vessels, which seem to reflect a development from indigenous traditions (**52**). Indeed the many inhumations and cremations from the mound reflect the traditional idea of special places for disposal of the dead. However, one of the inhumations was in a cist not unlike those used for burials of people with beakers. At North Mains, then, we can see all those components of burial the archaeologists of two generations ago thought went with beakers, except the beakers and associated artefacts themselves. An alternative hypothesis that beakers represent a cult or fashion among indigenous people is strengthened by this evidence, for plainly at least in this part of Perthshire there had been no take-over by people who believed the prestigious dead should be accompanied by beakers.

However, another great burial mound belonging in the same ten generations before 2000, at Collessie in Fife, seems to tell a different story. At the centre of the mound on the

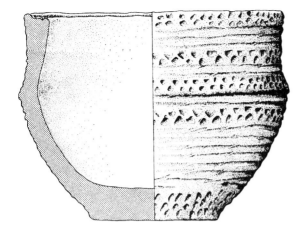

52 *Food vessels much like this one from Cowdenhill, in southern Scotland, were found accompanying burials set into the mound at North Mains, and with burials in the by-now ancient ceremonial enclosure nearby. Food vessels seem to be of indigenous origin, unlike beakers. They were used by many communities throughout the period that beakers were popular although, where both beakers and food vessels have been found together in cemeteries, beakers seem to have had higher status.*

old ground surface was a cist containing an inhumation and a beaker. Dug into the old ground surface were at least two pits. One contained a beaker. The other held a cremation with a bronze dagger, its haft decorated with a gold fillet (53). Remains of the ox-hide covering of its wooden sheath have provided the earliest date for a metal artefact from Scotland.

The south-east

Some things, however, seem not to have changed at all: further south, on the shores of the Forth, the great shell mounds at Nether Kinneil and Inveravon continued to accumulate. But at least there is the first radiocarbon-dated archaeological evidence for people in Lothian where, at Ruchlaw Mains in East Lothian, a simple inhumation with a beaker in a stone cist set in a grave has been dated to the centuries round 2000.

At Harehope by the Meldon Burn a burial, with many V-bored shale buttons and a belt-ring,

was placed in the centre of the cairn (54). It is the second-largest find of buttons from Britain, so the burial was unusually rich. There were also traces in the acid soil of several inhumations with beakers, although none of them is radiocarbon dated. Typologically the pots range from the supposedly earliest beakers to the supposedly latest.

53 *This bronze dagger blade found in a grave under a cairn at Collessie, in eastern Scotland, had become badly corroded by the time it was found. It was originally about 15cm (6in) long. The metal blade would have had a rounded top and a (probably wooden) hilt was riveted to it. The position of the bottom of the hilt, with its U-shaped indentation, can still be seen, as can part of one of the rivet holes. The handle had a pommel, bound by the gold band with its five horizontal grooves.*

54 Thirty-two conical shale buttons (thirty-one are shown here), an ovoid button and a belt-ring were found in the large grave-pit in the centre of the cairn at Harehope, in southern Scotland (see 45). Some of the buttons were heavily worn and others were fresh. The belt-ring and many of the buttons were decorated with ladder-patterns.

The cairn seems to have been used for a long time and it contains pottery of a kind which became common in the next period. Nevertheless, the evidence throws further doubts on the typological schemes so popular until the study by the British Museum. The fragment of pottery referred to in Chapter 4, and dated to between 3000 and 2500, recalls grooved-ware styles; and another pot from Harehope is associated with a cremation and decorated with incised V-marks in a fashion reminiscent of indigenous pottery. According to the typological schemes described at the beginning of this chapter, these would be the 'latest' beakers in the cairn. However, we could now see them as early and suppose they reflect local imitations of beakers. If this is what they were, we have more support for the idea that, in this area at least, beakers represent a fashion rather than invaders.

The great palisaded timber enclosure at Meldon Bridge, a few kilometres south down the narrow Meldon Water valley, near Peebles in the Borders, seems most likely to have been built towards the middle of this period. It shows that new ideas were being added to the repertoire of strategies with which people made a living at this time. Previously, with perhaps a peak of activity in the two or three centuries before 3000, small pits had been dug and used

to bury pottery and charred hazelnuts here. Now a high stockade was flung around two sides of a large area, the other two sides of which were provided by the Lyne Water and the Meldon Burn. The posts were tallest at the north-west corner, close to higher ground. Perhaps, then, the enclosure served a defensive purpose (55). There are very few signs of replacement of the stockade timbers, so presumably it stood for only a few generations.

Meldon Bridge is not unique. There is what seems to be a very similar enclosure at Forteviot in Perthshire. Both had one curious feature which suggests that they were not merely utilitarian enclosures, an avenue of substantial posts leading out from the enclosure. The avenue at Meldon Bridge seems to point to midsummer sunset. Perhaps ritual and prosaic use were mixed in a midsummer fair.

The south-west

At the settlement at Beckton, near Lockerbie, the latest radiocarbon date from the site comes from a crude oven. Since grooved ware had

55 The enclosure at Meldon Bridge, southern Scotland, was defined by a 3–4m (10–13ft) high stockade flung round two sides of a roughly rectangular 8ha (20 acre) area, the other two sides of which were provided by the Lyne Water (foreground) and the Meldon Burn. The posts were tallest, at about 4m (13ft), at the north-west corner. The avenue or entrance passage visible on the left-hand side of the enclosure was 4m (13ft) wide and over 25m (83ft) long. This reconstruction drawing omits some internal features which may be of different dates.

earlier been deposited on the site in small pits, it may not be too fanciful to see the ending of yet another grooved-ware settlement during the first ten generations after 2500.

Burnt mounds from near Crawford and from Stair Lodge in Galloway have been dated to the latter part of this period. Burnt mounds are composed of stones which have been heated in a fire and dropped into water troughs. Some are oval spreads or mounds of burnt stone; but some other mounds are roughly crescent-shaped, because stone was dumped around three sides of the water trough. In Orkney and Shetland these mounds can be very large, particularly when they lie next to or surround a house. Burnt mounds seem to go together with largely treeless landscapes; and it may be that those burnt mounds found on moorlands and marginal ground were hunting or herding camps, at which meat was boiled. Similar material has been found in Orkney, Shetland and the Western Isles in stone-built settlements. The point is that mounds and spreads of burnt stone often represent the heating of water, but so far it has not been possible to demonstrate what the water was heated for at any individual site.

The west

In Lanarkshire, near Thankerton, a tall adolescent was buried in a stone cist with a beaker, with simple cord decoration impressed into it, around the middle of the period 2500–2000.

It is just possible that settlements of roundhouses, built on small artificial platforms, had begun on the hillsides of Upper Clydesdale; they will be discussed in Chapter 6. Less doubt need attach to a burial, probably an inhumation, under a rough cairn at Fall Kneesend nearby. The cairn was probably contemporary with others at Fall Kneesend, which seem to represent laborious stone clearing of what is now a very marginal field. It is one of the few direct pieces of evidence from southern Scotland that even unfavourable pieces of

ground were being cleared at this time, and it also serves as a reminder that, at the same time as people were buried with beakers and food vessels, others were buried without durable goods.

The earliest dated burnt mound in Scotland belongs around the middle of this period. It lies on the slopes of Machrie Moor on Arran. It is perhaps evidence for hunting or herding. The timber circle at Machrie which had been built around 3000 and the lighter circular wicker or wattle fence surrounding it which had been built about 2500 were succeeded by a field system a few generations before 2000. The fields were divided up into plots by timber fences. Ploughing took place several times although few marks were recorded within the main timber circle. Judging by potsherds in a pit dug while the fields were still in use, both beakers and indigenous styles of pottery were in use at the same time as these field systems. The fields and the burnt mound may be related to a new pattern of settlement in Arran, which now or later included beaker-users in roundhouses.

Two rings of stubby stone overlying the fields cannot have been erected before 2250, yet one of them was set exactly over the site of an old circle which had been set up at least a dozen generations earlier (56). It seems the site was remembered long after the circle decayed (one post surrounded by a ring of stakes may have provided a material reminder) and throughout the period that beakers first became common in Scotland. This seems to argue not only for an adoption of beakers by indigenous people, rather than their being introduced by invaders, but also for survival of native traditions even after the introduction of a new cult, fashion or religion.

Among the sand-dunes at Ardnave on Islay the first of a succession of houses dating to the centuries around 2000 was set into the machair (the shell-sand fringing the coast). Like earlier houses, it was straight sided with round corners and an entrance at one end

56 *The two stubby stone circles at Machrie Moor, on Arran in western Scotland. Both were roughly 12 by 14m (40 by 46ft) across and built of stones varying around 1m (3ft) tall. The tallest stone was 1.5m (5ft) high. They were built on top of fields which had been divided up by hurdle fences, cultivated for barley with light wooden ploughs, and manured with seaweed. The fields were preceded by timber circles (see 46) and the holes in which these timbers were set are also visible in this excavation photograph.*

(**57**). The people who built it used food vessels. The house was much damaged and given the amount of remodelling which took place on the site other interpretations of its construction are possible. Indeed, there may have been several periods of use before it was replaced by a later house, also built by people using food vessels, which dates to the ten generations after 2000.

The last element in the complex skein of evidence reviewed here is provided by a burial at Sorisdale on Coll, with a beaker decorated all over by application of a twisted cord, which is one of the earliest in Scotland (and, indeed, in Britain). It belongs somewhere in the first twelve generations after 2500 (see **49**).

The fall

It does seem that the old social systems broke down a few generations after 2500, and it is all too tempting to ascribe this to the appearance of new people using beakers. Yet an overthrow by invaders of the society which built great ceremonial enclosures and used grooved ware would not explain what appears in the archaeological record. The available dates do not support frequent use of beakers until about 2300, and although the rich burials at Collessie could be quoted in support of ideas of a take-over by foreigners using beakers, most of the evidence is neutral or favours the idea that the funerary and ceremonial ideas represented by beakers and food vessels were adopted to fill a vacuum left by the disappearance of rituals involving the breaking of grooved-ware pots.

Admittedly, Meldon Bridge in the Borders, which was built at about the middle of this period, might be taken as evidence for defence against the sort of people who were buried with beakers at Harehope, a few kilometres up the Meldon valley, but at Harehope the hybrid pottery seems to support the idea of a gradual adoption of a fashion for beakers. On Orkney the few scraps of beaker from around the old settlements suggest transient occupation, while at Machrie Moor an old site was reused as if its original form and intention were remembered well after beakers came into fashion.

Elsewhere there seems to be evidence for introduction of food vessels. Their adoption could as easily be called evidence of an invasion as could the spread of beakers, yet they were based on indigenous pottery styles common in eastern and south-eastern Scotland (and northern England), and those who used them built at North Mains a monument quite as prestigious as anything associated with beakers.

There was no sudden deterioration in the climate. This leaves several possible explanations for the changes seen in this period: one is that the trend towards settlements in which many people lived together was disrupted by disease; yet another, perhaps the most significant for our own elaborate society, is that complex systems have the seeds of chaos built into them. Chance, in the form of a succession of seemingly trivial individual decisions and accidents, may have led to the disappearance of a potentially rich and stable society.

There are several good examples throughout the world of societies which reached this stage

57 *The walls at the back of this photograph are part of an earlier structure in the sand-dunes at Ardnave, on Islay in western Scotland, which measured at least 9m (30ft) long by 6.5m (22ft) across. The wall running half-way across the middle of the picture belongs to the house of this period; it seems to have inherited the wall at the bottom of the picture from the earlier structure. The living-space was at least 4.5m (15ft) long by 3.3m (11ft) wide and nearly straight sided, with round corners and an entrance in one end (at the left-hand side of this picture). Probably the older structure remained in use as a sort of yard.*

of development and then fell back into a simpler system. One, which has been well studied, is the Chaco Canyon culture of New Mexico. It is worth mentioning because the dry air there and the lack of subsequent disturbance have allowed far more evidence to survive on the surface than is readily available in Scotland. The Chaco Canyon culture had large settlements with Great Houses. It maintained strong connections between those settlements. It looks as if the people there incorporated some of their astronomical knowledge into the layout and relative siting of those centres. The Chaco Canyon culture built up to a peak; and then it collapsed over the next few generations. Although the coarseness of radiocarbon dating prevents our distinguishing between a collapse over a few generations and a more gradual change, it looks as if something similar happened in Scotland.

We have, then, perhaps part of an answer to the question posed earlier in this chapter. The old order with its centralizing tendencies collapsed for reasons we cannot properly explain and in its aftermath there was a period of considerable social fluidity and mobility. The idea of chieftains probably persisted and new leaders may have welcomed the new cult of beakers. Others encouraged the use of food vessels. The leaders of both those who used beakers and those who used food vessels reinforced their authority through new versions of old traditions. It is as if fairly small groups of communities were reinforcing their identities by a conscious difference from others. The houses of some of the population probably did not change much, judging by Ardnave, but towards the end of this period or the beginning of the next there was a considerable change, at least on Arran; roundhouses were built instead of the old straight-sided houses with rounded corners.

Stone circles from 3000 to 2000

There are no dates for the building of the great circular ditched enclosure and stone circle at Ring of Brodgar in Orkney, very close to Barnhouse, Stenness and Maes Howe, and far grander than the ditch and bank enclosure at Stones of Stenness. Like many other stone circles it was probably built at some time between 3000 and 2000 (**58**).

58 The Ring of Brodgar, in Orkney, consists of a circle of 60 stones inside a deep ditch with two entrance causeways across it. The stones, which are up to 4.5m (15ft) tall, define a true circle about 100m (more exactly, 340.7ft) across. It is the finest simple stone circle known (although its physical simplicity may arise from very complex ritual and social demands).

The problem of its date, however illuminating its solution might be for Orkney, is trivial compared to that of the dates of the stone rings of a broad area around Inverness and those of north-east Scotland. Pitglassie, which dated to the ten-generation period between 3750 and 3500, discussed in Chapter 2, had some of the simpler characteristics of these stone rings. It was roughly circular, included a setting of vertical posts (perhaps of timber rather than stone), and was used for cremations. The ring of close-set stones and the cremations at Raigmore, discussed in Chapter 4, only loosely dated, may also be an expression of the same ideas.

These stone circles fall into two broad groups, the Clava cairns of Inverness and the recumbent stone circles of the north-east.

At the type site for Clava cairns, Balnuaran of Clava, stone circles surround both round cairns, containing a chamber connected to the exterior by a passage, and a ring cairn with a small open central space (**59**). The stones of the circles are graded in height with the highest to the south-west. Probably at least some of the ring cairns pre-date some of the round cairns. Pitglassie shows circular cremation cemeteries were built

59 At Balnuaran of Clava, near Inverness in northern Scotland, there are two chambered cairns and a ring cairn each surrounded by a stone circle. Some of the stones of the cairns are decorated with cup-marks, and the stones of the circles are graded with the tallest to the south-west. These cairns are part of a linear cemetery extending along the valley floor.

very early in north-east Scotland, and there are many examples from the Kilmartin valley and from Perthshire of monuments which started life as enclosed spaces and ended as mounds. That said, many Clava ring cairns were never converted into mounds, and perhaps they represent a long-lived tradition within which, for a relatively short period, the practice of converting some to chambered mounds arose.

Many of the stone circles of north-east Scotland have one massive recumbent stone in the south-west quadrant, where the uprights of the stone circle are normally largest. On either side of the recumbent stone there is normally a pair of large upright flanking stones, as at the stone circle at Easter Aquhorthies (colour plate 9). The recumbent stones may have been designed to aid observation from the stone circle

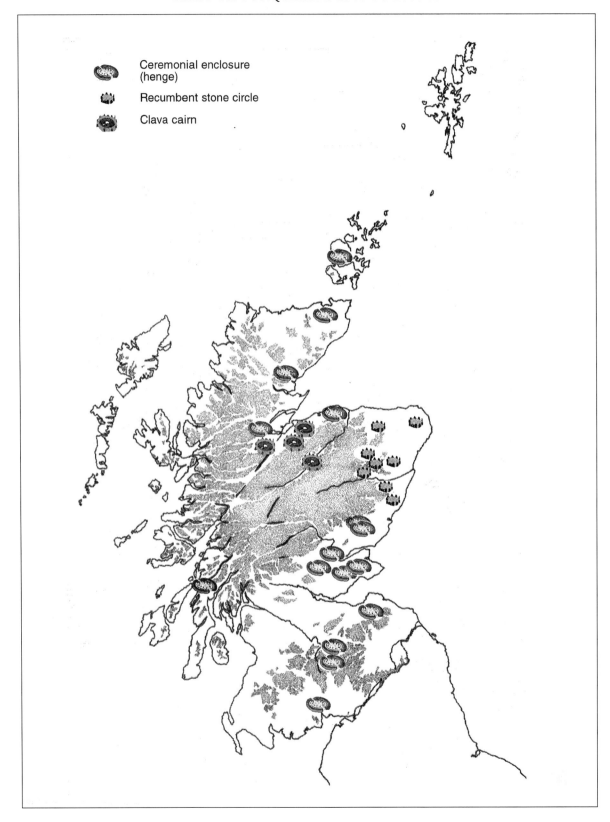

60 *The map gives a simplified impression of the distribution of three types of ritual monument which were probably built between about 3000 and 2000. The intention is to show where the types have been discovered, rather than how many there were. Thus one symbol may represent very few or many monuments. Henges (round enclosures, characterized by having a bank outside the encircling ditch), recumbent stone circles and Clava Cairns have different distributions. It has been suggested that this is because they were of much the same date but erected by groups with different rituals; but only a few of the henges and none of the others have been radiocarbon dated. Apart from some unusually large henges, which may reflect regional centralization of power in the centuries after about 3100, they probably represent local centres for rituals and burials.*

of the moon setting against the distant horizon at particular times of the year. If this is so we have a vivid illustration of the way prehistoric farmers integrated ceremonial with the sort of astronomy they will have practised to keep track of the seasons and regulate their ceremonies.

At some period of their existence – perhaps from the first – the recumbent stone circles and the Clava cairns were used for cremations. As we have seen, cremation was a normal way of disposal of the dead from 4000 onwards, and the origins of the earthen ceremonial henges of this period seem to be tied up with burial

practices. However, judging by the pottery and by the small kerb cairns found inside some of the recumbent stone circles, cremation continued at some of these sites through the second millennium.

Treacherous though distribution maps can be when used as aids to understanding the chronological relationships between the monuments of different areas, it may be that the reason why the distributions of henges and the stone circles of north-east Scotland are almost mutually exclusive is that they were built over the same period as each other (**60**). If they represented either different contemporary ideologies or regional variations in the expression of a powerful idea, that might explain why few henges were built in the north-east and why recumbent stone circles are not found further south along the east coast of Scotland. There seem to be regional groups of recumbent stone circles, in each of which the recumbents had a subtly different preferred direction. This suggests groupings of communities larger than a single settlement and gives us some idea of how society was organized in north-east Scotland. It is a large area in which at least religious beliefs were similar. Smaller groupings each had their own idiosyncrasies. Finally, individual settlements, or perhaps small groups of settlements, each had their own ceremonial site.

CHAPTER SIX

Villagers 2000 to 1500 BC

After 2000 the climate became more variable; oscillations over the next one thousand years must have made farming less predictable, but it was still warmer than or as warm as today. By now rough grazing, pastures and fields had replaced the ancient forest in many places. Still the land was a mosaic of different vegetation types, with an abundance of red deer and other wild animals. Hunting or herding was an important activity, since the burnt mounds found on the moors are most simply interpreted as camps where meat was cooked. There is abundant evidence of settlement with both small isolated houses and small settlements in which, for the first time, there are reliably dated roundhouses (**61**).

A patchwork of people

The general pattern seems to be that communities focused inwards. People made local choices about the burial rite and the kinds of pottery appropriate to their dead. Both cremations and inhumations were buried with beakers or food vessels, and cremations were placed in large urns. The earliest radiocarbon-dated Scottish hoard of metalwork contained beads dated to the centuries around 2000, and the next ten generations saw long-distance gift exchange or trade in metal tools and weapons and in jet, lignite and shale ornaments.

Shetland

In Shetland settlement continued at Scord of Brouster where the main house, Building 1, was in use at the beginning of this period. A new house, House 3, was built during the ten generations before 1500. Carbonized barley was recovered from it. A small settlement at Sumburgh airport, close to Jarlshof, was occupied; the first buildings were made of timber and the subsequent ones of stone. In an area of small fields at Tougs on West Burra there was an oval burnt mound with a small stone cooking-shed measuring 4 by 4m (13 by 13ft); it contained a water-boiling trough, in which cattle bones were found. At Mavis Grind a house like those at Scord of Brouster has been loosely dated to this period. Shetland was probably quite densely occupied; and it is clear that contacts with Orkney were strong in this period.

Orkney

A house (Structure 2) was built at Tofts Ness on Sanday around the middle of this period. It was much robbed, and like the earlier house there it seems to be part of a much larger (unexcavated) settlement. The pottery from it is comparable to that from Ness of Gruting on Shetland, which was built about 2000 and

61 *Map of sites radiocarbon dated to between 2000 and 1500.*

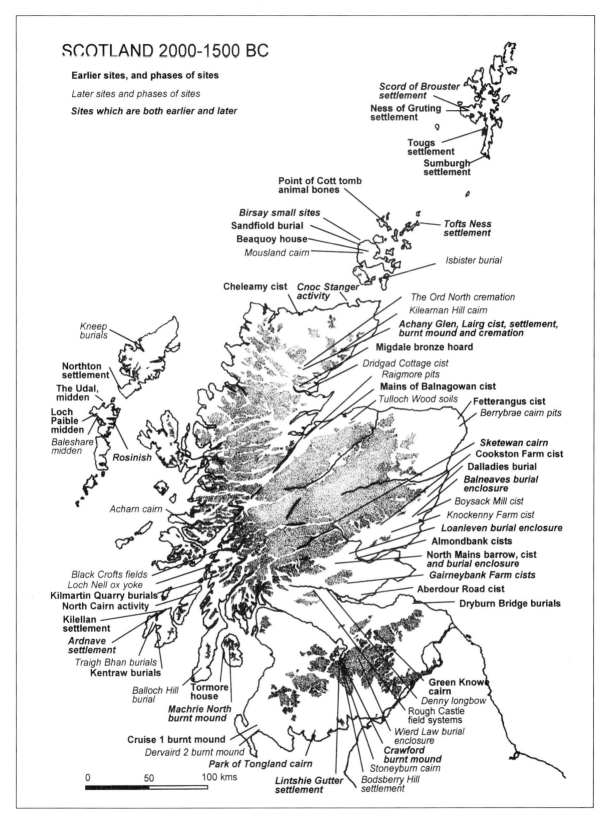

SCOTLAND 2000-1500 BC

Earlier sites, and phases of sites

Later sites and phases of sites

Sites which are both earlier and later

Scord of Brouster settlement

Ness of Gruting settlement

Tougs settlement

Sumburgh settlement

Point of Cott tomb animal bones

Birsay small sites

Sandfield burial

Beaquoy house

Mousland cairn

Tofts Ness settlement

Isbister burial

Cheleamy cist

Cnoc Stanger activity

The Ord North cremation

Kilearnan Hill cairn

Achany Glen, Lairg cist, settlement, burnt mound and cremation

Migdale bronze hoard

Dridgad Cottage cist

Raigmore pits

Mains of Balnagowan cist

Tulloch Wood soils

Fetterangus cist

Berrybrae cairn pits

Sketewan cairn

Cookston Farm cist

Dalladies burial

Balneaves burial enclosure

Boysack Mill cist

Knockenny Farm cist

Loanleven burial enclosure

Almondbank cists

North Mains barrow, cist and burial enclosure

Gairneybank Farm cists

Aberdour Road cist

Dryburn Bridge burials

Kneep burials

Northton settlement

The Udal, midden

Loch Paible midden

Baleshare midden

Rosinish

Acharn cairn

Black Crofts fields

Loch Nell ox yoke

Kilmartin Quarry burials

North Cairn activity

Kilellan settlement

Ardnave settlement

Traigh Bhan burials

Kentraw burials

Balloch Hill burial

Tormore house

Machrie North burnt mound

Cruise 1 burnt mound

Dervaird 2 burnt mound

Park of Tongland cairn

Green Knowe cairn

Denny longbow

Rough Castle field systems

Wierd Law burial enclosure

Crawford burnt mound

Stoneyburn cairn

Bodsberry Hill settlement

Lintshie Gutter settlement

0   50   100 kms

91

described in Chapter 5. Some of the pots had soapstone filler, again suggesting contacts with Shetland.

At Beaquoy, near Dounby, a small rectangular house, its inner space dominated by a huge cooking-trough, was abandoned at about this time (**62**). Around it had accumulated a burnt mound, forming a rough crescent with the house in its open hollow. Querns and ard shares suggest cereals were eaten. The building, surrounded by the heap of pot-boilers and with a peat stack close to its door, sat close to small fields in a landscape generally dominated by rough grazing and heather moors. Other large crescent-shaped burnt mounds in Orkney and Shetland probably also surrounded dwellings rather than special cooking-sheds.

The remarkable rock-cut tomb at Sandfiold near Skara Brae, first used in the period 2750 to 2500, was opened for insertion of another burial. By now the normal mode of burial in Orkney was cremation in low mounds and cairns; and the reuse of the rock-cut tomb at Sandfiold is perhaps yet another example of the long periods over which burial places were remembered throughout Scotland. This impres-

sion of links with the distant past is reinforced by the discovery of a polished stone axehead, next to a cist containing a cremation, in a low, neatly kerbed turf burial mound at Mousland in the west of the main island. It is usually assumed that stone axes went out of use at the end of the Neolithic. However, fine axeheads had a significance beyond their use as tools; and perhaps this one symbolized a long connection between a powerful family and the land.

The north

In Achany Glen near Lairg there was woodland clearance during the first ten generations after 2000 and a burnt mound started to accumulate. Judging by dates from a pit below it,

62 The house at Beaquoy in the middle of Orkney was about 6m (20ft) long by 3m (10ft) wide and surrounded by a mound of pot-boilers. In this photograph of the site under excavation many of the pot-boilers have been removed. The water-boiling pit has had half of its contents excavated. Baulks of earth and stone have been left unexcavated across the site, to maintain a record of the archaeological layers.

and others from the middle and top of the mound, it seems to have been used off and on for the next five hundred years. Further south in the Glen a small cairn was built, ending a long period of use of a small stony area for burials, involving mere scatters of cremated bone but some well-preserved artefacts. Towards the middle of this period the first house of what was to become a substantial settlement was built and, at some time during the next ten generations, a cremation burial was placed near the house and a cremation was inserted into the collapsed chambered tomb at The Ord, near Lairg, along with globular bowls. Although the acidity of Sutherland soils means that buried unburnt bones would soon dissolve, so inhumations would not survive to be found today, cremation was at least one normal way of disposing of the dead in the area south of Lairg.

During the ten generations from 1750 to 1500 a settlement of roundhouses flourished in Achany Glen (63). The houses were large, with conical roofs resting on circular walls of turf and stone and supported by a ring of posts. The area between the posts and the wall was not as worn by constant use as the rest of the floor. Perhaps it was used for storage or for sleeping-platforms. The people in this and the next period used quern stones for grinding grain, and simple stone-tipped ploughs. There is evidence of tillage nearby: organic waste (and a few accidentally incorporated artefacts) was spread on the fields, and plough soil washed downhill to rest against a substantial dyke. Resources other than pasture and ploughable land were available: despite the earlier clearance of trees in the Glen, undisturbed woodland survived on the plateau above the valley, only forty-five minutes' walk from the houses.

This settlement may have been the property of a few families or of a single extended family. The people will not have lived in all the buildings at any one time. Instead, each building went through a cycle of construction, occupation, and

63 *An air photograph of part of a settlement of several roundhouses in Achany Glen, near Lairg in northern Scotland, during excavation. Around the houses were ploughed fields beyond which was pasture, and further away still were areas of woodland. The settlement remained in use for many centuries.*

then use for other purposes such as storage or housing of animals, followed sometimes by reuse of the site for agriculture. These substantial houses show that there was considerable prosperity based on barley growing and grazing of animals, even if the durable goods found in the houses and the middens outside them seem to the modern eye monotonously plain. In the rest of Sutherland, as in Achany Glen, pockets of settlement seem to form the general pattern; one house of such a settlement on Kilearnan Hill has been dated to this period. The pattern established now was to last for four thousand years: 'I remember you would see a mile or half a mile between every town if you were going up the strath. There were four or five families in each of these towns, and hill pasture for miles, as far as they could wish to go. The people had plenty of flocks of goats, sheep ... and they were living happy, with flesh and fish and butter, and cheese' (Angus Mackay, quoted by Eric Cregeen in 1964).

The National Museum of Scotland dating-programme has produced a date of around 2000 for the wooden backing to a tubular bronze-coated bead from a hoard of tools and ornaments from Migdale in southern Sutherland. This is particularly significant because hoards and the moulds used for casting objects in the same bronzeworking tradition are concentrated in the area around Inverness and in north-east Scotland, suggesting local bronzeworking. Perhaps the hoard was buried as an offering to some god or natural force; that is a favoured explanation today, replacing the old idea that all hoards were buried to keep them safe. Be that as it may, the hoard could represent the personal belongings of a rich individual (**colour plate 10**).

The north-east and east

Further south and east, burials with beakers and food vessels were abundant. Burials with beakers of this period occurred at Mains of Balnagowan, near Fort George, and in the old earthen long barrow at Dalladies. A date in the ten-generation period before 1500 from a small embanked stone circle at Berrybrae in north-east Scotland may also reflect reuse of a sacred site of an earlier period, though if it were constructed between 2000 and 1500 that would not jar with the general pattern of local developments which seems to be emerging from the dated settlements and burials.

Further south again at North Mains, one of several cists was set in an unusually deep (1.6m/5ft) pit in the old ceremonial enclosure during the first part of this period. The body of a young woman was buried with a food vessel which contained gruel or a drink flavoured with meadowsweet. Altogether there were three burials with food vessels. Perhaps those who built the nearby massive mound recognized the sacred nature of the earlier site; but it may be that the proximity of the mound was the main reason why the burial was placed here. Three cremations in large urns suggest a ritual different at least in detail, as does a cremation in the later part of this period, placed in a shallow pit with a barbed and tanged arrowhead and other flints, most of them burnt.

There are many other burials and groups of burials with beakers or food vessels dated to this period in east Scotland. Some of them were enclosed by circular ditches, which may suggest that the burials were also covered by a low mound or enclosed by a bank. Other burials were not accompanied by pottery. A ring cairn was built at Sketewan in Perthshire at some time in the first half of this period, with a small subsidiary enclosure; and unaccompanied cremations were placed inside it. There is an impression of local variation, as if communities were making a selection from a wide range of possibilities within a tradition of successive single burials inside an enclosure formed by a ditch, bank or ring cairn.

Among the most remarkable individual finds in such a burial enclosure is a cist at Loanleven, for one of its sides was formed by a slab decorated with ring-marks in a style recalling the decorated outcrops of the Kilmartin area in Argyll, or the slabs from the chambered tomb at Pierowall in Orkney destroyed before 3000. The slab seems to have weathered in an upright position (**64**). Its reuse was a recognition of its sacred nature; but its burial was a rejection of the reasons why it was originally set up. What

64 *The cemetery at Loanleven in eastern Scotland was defined by a ditch 1.2m (4ft) wide and 0.65m (2ft) deep enclosing an area about 20m (66ft) across. Inside it were cists containing burials and cremations. The damaged decorated slab shown here had been reused as the side of one of the cists. It was 1.6m (slightly over 5ft) long. The ring-marks and 'looking-glass' on it were produced by pecking with a hammer.*

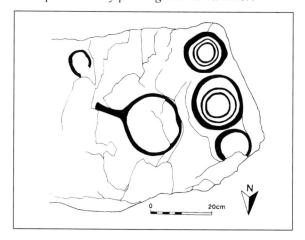

had been set up under the sky was now concealed in the earth. A few sherds of food vessel were retrieved from the cemetery during its destruction by quarrying and a cist with fragments of a food vessel was placed in the enclosure during the centuries round 1500.

Yet another variation is seen at Balneaves in Angus, where a penannular ditch enclosed a burial area. There were seven cremation burials inside the enclosure, four of them in large urns, some plain and others crudely decorated (65). At some time there may have been one or more standing stones inside the enclosure, because a slab over 2m (6ft) long was found there in a modern pit (one way of clearing the land for agriculture in early modern times was to bury large stones), but since all the burials were neatly inside the ditch, and all the dates were similar to each other, the excavator interpreted the site as a purpose-built cemetery rather than an older enclosure reused for burials.

Some cemeteries seem never to have been enclosed. Five cists have been found at Gairneybank Farm in Kinross, spread out over a distance of 50m (166ft), and they included burials with a beaker and food vessels (66). The earlier of the two dated burials was accompanied only by a joint of pork and the other by a food vessel. At Almondbank near Perth there was a mixture of burial rites. One cremation was accompanied by a food vessel, while an inhumation also dated to this period was placed below a cist in the filling of which was a simple jet necklace.

The south

In the areas to the south of the Forth the burials were equally various. Two sets of double inhumations were placed in cists at Dryburn Bridge in Lothian, one with a beaker placed on its capstones, and two unaccompanied cremations were found in a single pit at the cairn at Harehope. In the Borders at Weird Law a smaller and simpler version of the ring cairn at Sketewan was built: the circular enclosure defined by a low bank was used for many single cremations in small pits.

At Park of Tongland in Dumfries and Galloway four cremations, two of them in burial urns, date to the ten generations after 2000.

65 The burial enclosure at Balneaves, in eastern Scotland, was defined by a ditch about 1.7m (6ft) across and up to 0.5m (less than 2ft) deep, enclosing an area about 7m (23ft) across. The entrance was 2.5m (8ft) wide. Four of the cremations inside it were in burial urns, two decorated and two plain.

66 The burial cists forming the cemetery at Gairneybank, in eastern Scotland, were inserted into a low natural gravel ridge over a distance of about 48m (160ft). Two of the cists contained burials with food vessels, one contained a beaker and another a burial with a decorated bowl and small flat bronze knife with a riveted handle. This skeleton, which was in yet another cist, was accompanied by a joint of pork.

67 These pots, found with the cremations in the cemetery at Park of Tongland, in south-western Scotland, included a plain urn with a slight bulge, quite possibly designed so a skin cover could be tied over its top, and an urn with decoration perhaps mimicking lashings used to fasten a skin cover to domestic pots. The pots are similar to some of those found on contemporary settlements.

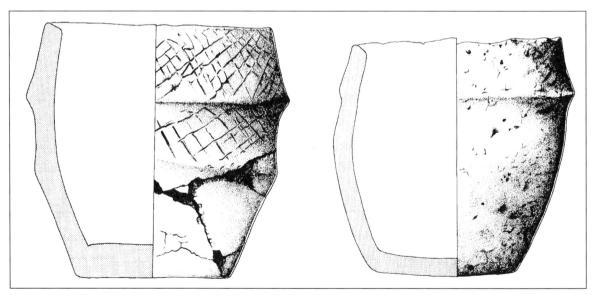

68 *The wall of the house on Platform 13 at Lintshie Gutter, in western Scotland, was defined by two ring-grooves, one about 8m (26ft) across and the other 9m (30ft) across. The area between them may have been filled with turf. The roof was supported by a ring of posts. The house seems to have had a front and a side entrance, one of which was protected by a substantial porch. This artist's impression gives some idea of what it may have looked like.*

One coarse plain urn, with a collar, had a small plain pot in it (**67**). Given the finds from Lintshie Gutter, described below, it does seem quite likely that the urns were similar to those used in contemporary settlements. During the ten generations before 1500 more pits were dug and abundant charcoal was scattered in the body of the overlying crudely kerbed cairn. It seems the local practice had become very thorough cremation, leaving no traces of bone. Before the cairn was built at least two small standing stones were erected, sticking about 1m (3ft) above ground; and two more were put up at the same time as the cairn.

Burnt mounds at Cruise in south-west Scotland and at Crawford, in Clydesdale, date to the earlier part of this 500-year period, and others at Dervaird and Glenluce in south-west Scotland and at Machrie on Arran date to the latter half. They suggest that hunting or herding in marginal areas was an important part of the societies of the south-west and west.

The west

At Lintshie Gutter there are 31 known platforms ranging along the north-facing side of the hill. Slightly more than half the platforms are in a cluster to the west of a small burn while the rest form a straggle on the east side. All the excavated platforms were part of this straggle. A shallow hearth, outlined with heat-reddened stones, was used outside the house on Platform 13. It is the earliest safe date from the platform settlement, although one of those obtained from another platform did fall in the previous period and it is possible the settlement started before 2000. Platform 13 and the house on it had been much damaged by ploughing, but enough of the house-plan was recovered to suggest it was built of turf and soil within wattle and daub wall-faces, and that it had a substantial porch over its entrance (**68**).

During the next ten generations, the structures on Platforms 1 and 5 were in use. The building on Platform 1 was not a house. Instead it seems to have served as a byre, or a pound for cattle or sheep. That on Platform 5 was a roundhouse with a substantial wall of soil and turf between wattle and daub wall-faces, and a ring of stout internal posts supported a heavy conical roof. The house had two entrances. Inside it, near where it backed on to the hillside, was a substantial oven (**69**). The house contained a quern and remains of both small and large plain pots, some with cordoned necks. Many showed signs of having been used for cooking. Some of this pottery is like the burial urns from Park of Tongland and Balneaves.

Further south near Bodsberry Hill one platform of another settlement has been dated to this same ten generations before 1500. It held

69 *The structure on Platform 5 at Lintshie Gutter, in western Scotland, was built on a platform. The rear of the platform was cut 2.5m (8ft) down into the hill slope, and its front was formed by piling up the material quarried from the back. On it was built a roundhouse 9m (30ft) across with two entrances through a wattle-lined wall. A ring of posts supported the roof. Inside the house were found the remains of an oven. This artist's impression gives an idea of the large range of activities which may have taken place inside the building – and reminds us that the people used many tools and receptacles made of organic materials which do not survive on dry sites like Lintshie Gutter.*

a small roundhouse, like those on some of the platforms at Lintshie Gutter but, in this case, with stone foundations. There seems little doubt that Upper Clydesdale was heavily occupied by peasant farmers, some richer than others, during this and subsequent periods.

A date for a burial in one of three small low cairns at Stoneyburn in Clydesdale, not far from Lintshie Gutter, provides another illustration of reuse of ancient sacred sites. What is extraordinary in this case is the inconspicuousness of the cairns and the fact that the largest of the three had been built precisely over a presumably long-abandoned Neolithic pit. It is evidence for long-surviving traditions inherited by people like those who lived in the platform settlement at Lintshie Gutter.

A roundhouse was built at Tormore in the west of Arran, not far from Machrie Moor, during the first ten generations after 2000. Its wall was made of stony soil lined internally with a wattle fence. Inside was a ring of stout posts which supported a wattle and turf roof (**colour plate 11**). The pottery found in it was beaker, decorated all over with horizontal lines. Apart from the insecurely dated roundhouse at Dunloskin Wood in Argyll, which may have been built as early as the period 3500–3250, this and the house on Platform 13 at Lintshie Gutter are the earliest firmly dated true roundhouses. Obviously, since we have so few properly dated settlements we must be careful not to put too much weight on the evidence, but at the moment it does seem that a change in the commonest building shape, from straight-sided buildings with rounded corners to roundhouses, may have started in the centuries following 2000.

One of the many exciting results of the National Museum's dating programme is the placing of an ox yoke from Loch Nell in the period between 2000 and 1500 (**70**). This is the earliest direct evidence for animal traction, for it is conceivable that the rip ards which produced the plough-marks of earlier periods were pulled by people. Also from Argyll come dates for charcoal under field walls at Black Crofts, Connel, where later a raised bog was to engulf the fields. As elsewhere in mainland Scotland (with the usual proviso, that cremated bone survives much better than unburnt bone in acid soils) cremation seems to have been the normal

burial ritual. Examples are known from the gravel terraces of the Kilmartin valley, from Acharn in Morvern, with a pinhead or bead, and from Balloch Hill, Kintyre. There, where a hill-fort was later to be built, there were two cremations in urns under a slight mound, with a decorated miniature vessel, a charred pine or spruce dish and a rough pendant. The dish serves as a salutary reminder that in much of Scotland household dishes and bowls may often have been made of wood.

On Islay there was yet another variant within the burial traditions of the earlier part of this period. A clay-luted cist at Kentraw was found to contain between four and six burials with a food vessel and a decorated miniature pot. At Traigh Bhan in Islay, somewhat later in date than Kentraw, the burial ritual was again inhumation in a cist, and the practice of more than one burial in the same cist seems to have continued, because around 1500 or at most a few generations later another inhumation was added, with a food vessel. Although, as the burials at Dryburn Bridge in south-east Scotland show, cists were occasionally used for multiple burials on the mainland of Scotland, there is a suggestion of a strong and distinctive local tradition on Islay with some echoes of the burial practices of the farmers of the period before 3000.

On Islay, as elsewhere in this period, the pots placed with burials were not much different

70 *The ox yoke from Loch Nell, in western Scotland, was found in a peat-moss. It would have been used to harness two beasts to a plough. It is now 1.05m (a little over 3ft) across and, even though it will have been larger before it dried out, the oxen which it fitted must have been small.*

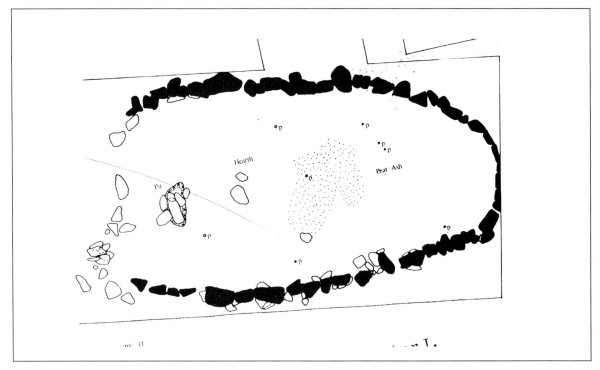

Hearth

Pit

Peat Ash

from those used in the settlements. A new house was built at Ardnave during the first ten generations after 2000, inside the remains of the old one. Again the pottery in it was food vessel. The house continued in occupation into the latter part of this period, for we have dates from a layer with abundant cattle bones.

The Western Isles

Meanwhile in the Western Isles fields were cultivated by people who used beaker pottery. At Rosinish, on the edge of one of the sounds which separates the islands of Benbecula and North Uist, there was abundant evidence of cultivation close to fragmentary remains of a lightly built house. Probably the marks left in the sand were made by an ard or by a single-tine harrow.

At Northton, on Harris, two houses were built at about this time (71). The area had been occupied in the period 3250 to 3000, when there was a rich range of natural resources (and domesticated foodstuffs). Now, too, the sea provided a varied harvest: lobsters,

71 Excavation showed that what survived of the better-preserved of the two houses at Northton, in the Western Isles, was a stone-lined oval hollow about 8.5m long by slightly more than 4m wide (28 by 14ft). Inside it was a hearth. The entrance was at one end. Perhaps it held back the sand from a light hut or tent less than 3m (about 9ft) wide.

crabs, urchins, limpets (perhaps used for bait), seal, walrus and several species of sea-bird. The land provided red deer (some with enormous antlers) and there were roughly equal amounts of cattle and sheep or goat bones from the site (implying cattle were a more important food resource since each beast provides much more food than a sheep). Leatherworking and potting took place. However, there was no evidence for cultivation – no grain and no querns.

Rosinish and Northton show two different aspects of the economy of the people who used beakers for most of this period. The settlements may have been seasonal; certainly the buildings at both sites were lightly built and may even have been roofed with skins.

Inhumation seems to have been at least one of the rituals in use in the Western Isles for there was a burial in the shell-sand dunes at Cnip headland in Lewis.

Prosperous communities

The period 2000 to 1500 seems to be characterized by small prosperous communities led by petty chieftains. Although there was little evidence for the precise way in which agriculture was carried out it seems that ploughs pulled by oxen were used to rip up pasture, and either light harrows or hand tools were used to create seedbeds. Barley was the most common grain. Many houses on the mainland were now round in plan; but in the western and northern islands they were still straight sided with round corners. The first large lowland settlements were built, some on groups of hillside platforms.

In their burial practices communities appear to have made local choices drawing on old traditions. The practice of burying people in roughly circular enclosures had origins, in north-east Scotland at least, in the period between 3750 and 3500. It seems by now to have been (and may have been in all the eastern parts of Scotland since the last long barrows were built in the period between 3500 and 3000) a normal way to dispose of the dead. A parallel tradition of single burials in cists had perhaps become common around 2500, although some of the latest burials in chambered tombs were in shallow pits and the practice of burying individuals in distinct graves may go back beyond 3000. Yet in parts of Scotland even quite small cists were sometimes used for multiple burials.

There are no radiocarbon dates for the cairns forming the linear cemetery in the Kilmartin valley in Argyll, but it is likely that they were used over a very long period. The chambered cairn at Nether Largie South, reused for burials with beakers and other pottery, was probably built before 3000, and there is clear evidence from the Glebe Cairn and from Nether Largie North that those cairns were preceded by roughly circular enclosures. The axeheads carved on a massive cist slab decorated with cup-marks and axeheads under the cairn at Nether Largie North in the Kilmartin valley look much like the axeheads in the Migdale hoard dated to around 2000. So do similar carvings on a slab used to build a cist at Ri Cruin, at the southern end of the linear cemetery. Although these stones may have been reused from earlier settings, the linear cemetery was probably completed by 1500.

The hoard of bronze tools and ornaments at Migdale dates to about 2000. Products and stone moulds from the same metalworking tradition are found throughout Britain, although more than half come from an area between Angus and southern Sutherland. Some of the jet ornaments found in Scotland were made of jet obtained from near Whitby in Yorkshire (although many similar objects were made of more local shales and lignites, such as those which outcrop near Brora in Sutherland). In this period, then, there were long-distance connections and trading or exchange networks.

CHAPTER SEVEN

Mastering the land
1500 to 1000 BC

Hard times

Undefended settlements and intensifying agriculture characterize this period (72). Towards the end the climate became for a while similar to that of today before it deteriorated to become even wetter and cooler by 750. Blanket peat growth started or accelerated in many areas. In Shetland, Orkney and Jura, people had already had to battle against wet and wind for many generations. With careful soil management they could survive; but the evidence reviewed below shows that these efforts sometimes failed before the end of this period. By way of contrast, there is a strong impression of agricultural intensification at least in eastern Scotland, as if the population were still growing and its response to worsening conditions was vigorous and effective for at least a while.

Shetland and Orkney

There is little dated evidence for what was happening in Shetland during the first ten generations of this period although barley has been found in a midden underlying a much later broch at Pool of Virkie, in the bay to the north-east of Jarlshof.

However, during the ten generations before 1000 a house was built at Tougs, Burra, close to the burnt mound of the period 2000–1750 discussed in Chapter 6 (73). Externally it was large, but it had very thick walls. Projecting stones created alcoves around a central space in a way familiar from the houses of the (undated) Bronze Age village at Jarlshof. Although peat was growing in the neighbourhood, the evidence of pollen and abundant stone ploughshares shows cereal was grown around the house.

As in Shetland, so in Orkney, there is only limited evidence for activity in the two or three centuries after 1500. At St Boniface on the west coast of Papa Westray, evidence of settlement was revealed during an excavation which focused on later structures. An ox yoke found at the White Moss is direct evidence for animal traction. Towards 1000, however, a house surrounded by pot-boilers was abandoned at Liddle Farm in South Ronaldsay and another was built at Tofts Ness on Sanday.

The house at Liddle was egg-shaped, and round it ran a path with a low wall between it and a mound of pot-boilers (74). Inside a double-skinned wall was a flagged floor in which were set a hearth and a monumentally proportioned trough. Slabs set in from the walls of the house defined compartments which were too small to be sleeping-places. It is tempting to see them as places where people sat during feasting. The pots from the house were plain and flat bottomed. Although

72 *Map of sites radiocarbon dated to between 1500 and 1000.*

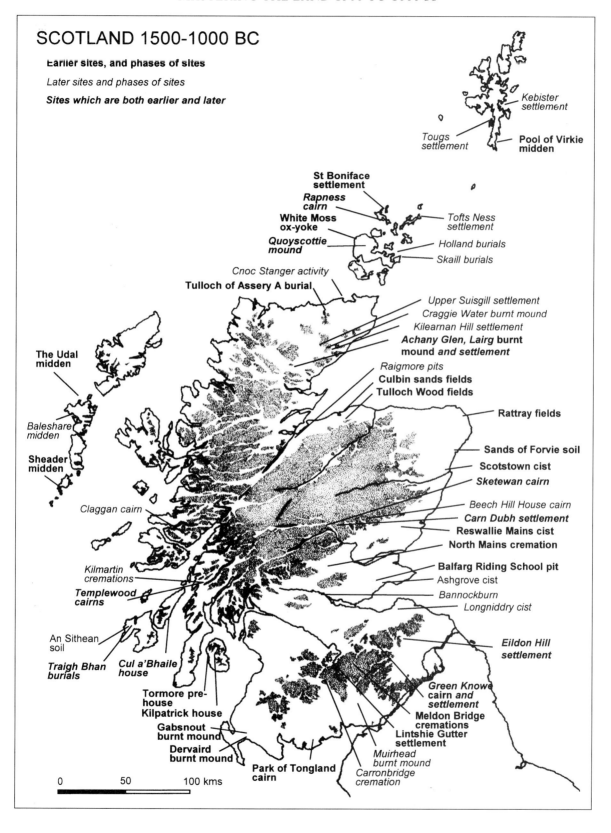

SCOTLAND 1500-1000 BC

Earlier sites, and phases of sites

Later sites and phases of sites

Sites which are both earlier and later

Kebister settlement

Tougs settlement
Pool of Virkie midden

St Boniface settlement
Rapness cairn
White Moss ox-yoke
Quoyscottie mound

Tofts Ness settlement
Holland burials
Skaill burials

Cnoc Stanger activity
Tulloch of Assery A burial

Upper Suisgill settlement
Craggie Water burnt mound
Kilearnan Hill settlement
Achany Glen, Lairg burnt mound and settlement

The Udal midden

Raigmore pits
Culbin sands fields
Tulloch Wood fields

Rattray fields

Baleshare midden

Sands of Forvie soil
Scotstown cist
Sketewan cairn

Sheader midden

Beech Hill House cairn
Carn Dubh settlement
Reswallie Mains cist
North Mains cremation

Claggan cairn

Balfarg Riding School pit
Ashgrove cist

Kilmartin cremations
Templewood cairns

Bannockburn
Longniddry cist

An Sithean soil

Eildon Hill settlement

Traigh Bhan burials
Cul a'Bhaile house

Green Knowe cairn and settlement
Meldon Bridge cremations
Lintshie Gutter settlement

Tormore prehouse
Kilpatrick house
Gabsnout burnt mound
Dervaird burnt mound

Muirhead burnt mound
Carronbridge cremation

Park of Tongland cairn

0   50   100 kms

73 *The house at Tougs, or Sunnybank, in Shetland (in the foreground of this photograph), was quite large externally, measuring 13 by 8.5m (43 by 28ft). Its thick walls are indicated by spreads of small stones. The large stones formed the inner wall-faces, and projecting stones created alcoves round a central space, well under 6m (19ft) across. In the background is an earlier mound of burnt stones, which had been used as pot-boilers to heat up water. To its right are the remains of a small house containing a trough in which water was heated.*

74 *The stone-built house at Liddle in South Ronaldsay, in Orkney, had walls over a metre broad defining a living-space about 6m (20ft) long by 4m (13ft) wide. Inside was a water trough 1.6m (5ft) long and 1m (3ft) deep. Stones about 1m tall, set against the inner wall-face, defined compartments about 1m wide. The photograph shows it after the mound of pot-boilers around it had been excavated away. The wall furthest to the right had held back that mound.*

ploughshares were found on the site it did not produce any querns, so perhaps cereals were not processed there; but traces of cereal pollen found in one of the dated deposits suggest that the house formed only one part of a community's resources.

At a similar date a large roundhouse with a double-wall construction and radial divisions was built at Tofts Ness on Sanday. In the central area were a hearth and two stone-built drains. Next to the roundhouse was a small oval house, with a clay-luted stone tank occupying much of its central space. There were few burnt stones, so although the house was shaped like that at Liddle its function may have been different. There is abundant evidence of cultivation on Tofts Ness from the Neolithic onwards. It is, hardly surprisingly, difficult to date the soils except after this period when a sand-blow covered much of the area to a depth of 0.2m (6in) or more. It does seem, however, that turves were imported on to the infield to provide a thick topsoil, and midden was spread on the fields.

Towards the middle of this period cremations were placed in a low, broad burial mound at Quoyscottie, in the middle of the main Orkney island. Both inhumation and cremation were practised in Orkney during the following ten generations. People were buried at Holland on a headland east of Kirkwall, while in addition to further cremations set into the low mound at Quoyscottie, burnt human bone was placed under the central slab of a large but low burial cairn at Rapness on Westray. If the typical burials of the period were large low mounds and cairns with pockets of cremated bone, it is unlikely that much evidence for them will survive, for they are very vulnerable to ploughing.

The north

The only dated evidence from Caithness is a crouched burial in the collapsed remains of the ancient burial place at Tulloch of Assery. Given that cremation was the usual burial rite by now, it is a useful reminder that the two different ways of disposing of bodies seem to have been used in Scotland throughout prehistory.

On the mainland, charcoal from the burning of a house at Suisgill in the Strath of Kildonan shows that it was constructed between 1250 and 1000. Lightly built of wood, it may have been as much as 10m (33ft) across, although not all of its circuit survived. There was evidence for a succession of earlier phases. At the base of the sequence was a plough soil; then came an earlier house, unlikely to date before the previous period 1500–1250, followed by more cultivation. The importance of this site lies not only in the evidence for ploughing and lightly built wooden houses in an area where most of the surface evidence is for stone-built structures, but also in its preservation below deposits drifting downslope. On the flat land of the river valley later agriculture will have destroyed much evidence and it is near the base of the valley slopes that we can expect to find the best evidence for the Highland way of life during the prehistoric period.

The settlement of roundhouses in Achany Glen south of Lairg continued to flourish although the earliest house, House 2, was abandoned. The largest house in the settlement, House 4, was built at the end of the previous period or towards the beginning of this one. It burnt down probably before the end of this period, and fire-cracked stones which seem to represent the same cooking technique as that seen at burnt mounds were found overlying the wall. During the ten generations before 1000 a new house, House 6, was built on the infield (75). Two burnt mounds a few hundred metres from the settlement were in use, and perhaps the people of the settlement heated water there for some activity which had to take place away from the houses. It may be, however, that people from other communities herded their animals or hunted here, for the settlement seems to have been abandoned finally at some time between 1250

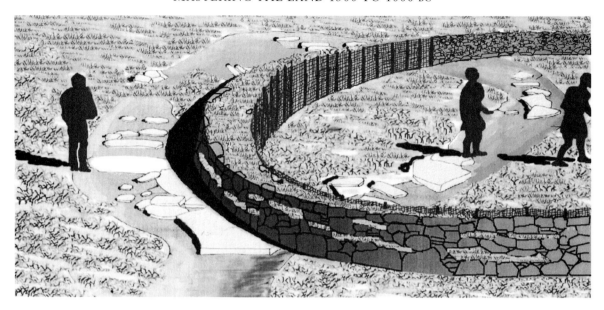

75 *This diagram reconstructs the shape of House 6 in the settlement in Achany Glen near Lairg, in northern Scotland, and shows its relationship to an earlier house. That earlier house had been almost completely ploughed away before House 6 was built. All that remained of it were depressions worn in its floor just inside its walls, and the slabs and earth used to level the depressions. House 6 may not have been a dwelling-place but have served some other function in the community. It, too, was ploughed in its turn and its walls survived only as low ridges of stone and earth. It may originally have had a stone and turf outer wall-face as indicated here but, if so, it was robbed away and used in still-later houses. The wall may instead have been built largely of turf.*

and 1000. Nevertheless there was much scrub clearance and agricultural activity right through this latter period and probably settlement continued elsewhere in the valley.

The north-east

At Rattray, near the coast at the tip of north-east Scotland, a chance discovery gives sound information about field systems of this period on land covered by blown sand. There was an open grassy sand-plain along this bit of coast, with shrubby willow and hazel growing nearby. The local climate was damp. If, as the excavator suggested, a plough or harrow was used in preparing a seedbed rather than for ripping a grass cover before hoeing, it may be that the fields were used year after year, which would have left them very vulnerable to the wind. Indeed, the sand which smothered the site may reflect wind erosion from open fields nearby. However, the site is also of interest because a wattle hurdle at the edge of the field had been charred and detail of its construction survived. Since there were no signs of stake-holes to support a fence it may have been laid to provide a walkway (**76**).

There are very similarly dated middens at Culbin Sands further west along the coast, and at Sands of Forvie, north of Aberdeen, where ard-marks were preserved under a later cairn. Fragments of pottery at Rattray and Culbin Sands suggest the fields were fertilized with household refuse; the plain crude jars and flat-bottomed bowls were very broadly of the same kind as at Lintshie Gutter. This, then, seems to be the common form of agriculture on light, sandy soils near the coast. There is no sign of agricultural ridging, and the ground was prepared with a simple plough.

There is also evidence for agriculture at Tulloch Wood, an upland area near the margin of modern cultivation on the hill slopes

overlooking the Moray Firth near Kinloss. Here agriculture had taken place since 2500 and it seems that the many small cairns surviving in part of the area surveyed went with that earlier system of cultivation. Now, however, the fields were divided up by banks of stone and earth, creating long, wide strips of land (77). What limited evidence there is suggests that the fields were used to grow barley at least part of the time. There are remains of

76 *Ard-marks at Rattray, in north-eastern Scotland, were created by a plough or single-tine harrow with a U-shaped tip about 7mm (¼in) across. The ard-marks were 0.1–0.3m (4–12in) apart. Part of a wattle fence or walkway was preserved because it had been charred and then covered swiftly by blown sand. In this photograph part of it has been excavated away to show its relationship to the ard-marks.*

77 *The fields at Tulloch Wood, in north-eastern Scotland, were about 100–150m (330–500ft) wide. The walls dividing them (labelled as axial banks) run sideways on this plan and the other walls, running up and down the plan, may be of different date. The circular features are the walls of roundhouses. Where their relationship to the fields can be determined they are definitely later. The black dots are field-clearance cairns. The other lines show modern features. Although the length of the fields was not determined by excavation, they must have been very large.*

roundhouses in the fields, but some at least seem to be Iron Age in date, going with a reorganization of the field layout.

This is an important discovery, for although similar large fields are known in southern England none has until now been dated to this period in Scotland. They fit in with the idea of agricultural intensification. Plough animals must have been very necessary to deal with such large areas; and, conversely, large areas would be needed to grow crops to feed the plough animals or for their grazing.

The east

The settlement at Carn Dubh, or Tulloch Field, in north-east Perthshire, sits on an old river terrace and consists of six or seven roundhouses. Two of them are on artificial platforms. One of the houses was built towards the end of this period or the beginning of the next. The living-space was large and enclosed within a stout stone wall with a wide entrance to the south-west (78). Parts of a coarse bucket-shaped pot were found in the house. At least one of the other dwellings, however, was built much later – perhaps as late as the period after 500. Perhaps it would be better to see a succession of structures rather than a settlement of several houses. As in previous centuries, then, the pattern in the uplands was made up of individual households, each with its area of infield, and an economy based on livestock as much as cereals.

A funeral pyre was lit in the middle of the ring cairn at Sketewan, and the interior of the ring was filled with stones to form a large but low cairn. At Stone Wood in Perthshire a burial and pot were placed in a small stone circle with stones graded in size from north-east to south-west, a building tradition going back at least twenty and perhaps more than forty generations. The pot was generically similar to those found in the fields at Culbin Sands and Rattray of this period, and reminiscent of the pottery dated to before 3000 in the ancient enclosure at Kinloch Farm, Collessie in Fife. Bodies were cremated in the hollows left by four old pits close to the ancient ceremonial enclosure at North Mains, and neat stone settings placed round at least two of them. A pit full of charred barley at Balfarg Riding School reinforces this picture of ritual activity on and

78 *This diagram shows what the walls of the earliest house excavated at Carn Dubh, in eastern Scotland, may have looked like. Although they were over 3.5m (11ft) thick in places, they survived to far less a height than shown here. The area enclosed was about 14.5 by 10m (48 by 33ft).The diagram shows posts where post-holes were found; they do not help to show whether the whole of the inner area was roofed. The inner faces of the walls may have been lined with wattle. Lines of posts ran along the outer faces near the wide entrance. The space inside the walls was no doubt used, perhaps for storage or for sleeping. Two field walls run off from the house to the right.*

close to ancient ceremonial places. Food vessels were still in use in Perthshire: one was found with a cremation at Reswallie Mains and another with bronze and bone pins at Beech Hill House. A crude beaker containing gruel or a drink flavoured with meadowsweet was probably placed with an inhumation at Ashgrove in Fife during this period. The diversity seen in the previous period seems to have survived into this one.

The south-east

At Grainfoot in East Lothian two inhumations were placed in a large cist, one buried with a pork joint. Bodies were buried in cists in the Lothians in the subsequent periods from 1000 to the beginning of the Christian era, and it looks from the evidence from Dryburn Bridge in the previous period and from Grainfoot that inhumation had remained the usual burial ritual in Lothian.

Right next to Harehope cairn in the Borders is a small platform settlement called Green Knowe, where a roundhouse was built a century or so either way of 1500. The house wall was faced with wattle, like the walls of houses on the earlier platforms at Lintshie Gutter in Clydesdale. A shallow pit towards the front of the house was used for cooking. Pottery from the settlement was to include urns with collars later in this period; but most pots were quite crudely made simple jars like those on so many other sites of this time. Here at least the kind of pottery used for burials seems to have been fancier than that used domestically, for a small neatly decorated urn, containing a cremation and a small pot, was placed in the nearby Harehope cairn.

During the second half of this period three roundhouses were built one after the other on Platform 2. The doorway in the south-east was protected by a porch (**79**), and rubbish had been piled outside it to the left as if tossed there by a right-handed person. The abundant pottery varied in size. The larger jars had collars

79 *This platform at Green Knowe, in southeastern Scotland, supported a house about 10m (33ft) across, with a porch over a doorway (bottom left in this photograph). A slot (back left) which held the uprights for the rear wall of the house is just visible. The excavation trench in the foreground shows how the rubble, extracted from the rear of the platform, was piled downslope to create the platform.*

suggesting that they were designed so cloth or leather covers could be tied over them, and they were probably used for storage. Smaller vessels may have been used for drinking. A saddle quern was used for grinding seeds and grain, and there were many stone pounders and grinders. A stone with a shallow cup worked into it was probably used for grinding small amounts of colouring matter or medicinal seeds. Fragments of a shale pendant and ring show that the people traded for ornaments.

A few field banks which may be approximately contemporary ran down from the settlement to the Meldon Burn, on the other side of which was an even larger platform settlement of 18 houses and other structures. It looks as if the occupation of this sheltered valley was either dense or long-lived. Green Knowe itself with its nine platforms may have contained as many as forty to fifty people if all the platforms were used for houses; but as excavation at Lintshie Gutter has shown, some platforms may have been used to house animals and it is possible that the settlement held only one or two extended families.

80 *The small neat kerb cairn (the ring of small stones set edge to edge) in the centre of the stone circle at Temple Wood in the Kilmartin valley of western Scotland, could be thought of as a miniature roundhouse for the dead. It was about 3m (10ft) across. The massive cist contained cremated human bones. The rubble around the kerb conceals the remains of three other burial places, one seemingly earlier and two of about the same date as this one. Excavation showed that an earlier arrangement of the one shown here, and one of the others, had what look remarkably like miniature blocked-off doorways.*

At the south end of the valley leading up from Peebles to Green Knowe, burials were placed in a small cemetery at Meldon Bridge, where the great palisaded enclosure had been. A curious variant on normal burials was found here: a cremation had been placed in a small tunnel dug into the side of a pit.

The south-west and west

Burnt mounds were still in use in the south-west at Muirhead near Lockerbie and in the Rhinns of Galloway at Gabsnout, showing that even if agriculture dominated the eastern lowlands hunting or herding was an important part of the economy elsewhere. At Park of Tongland yet another cremation was laid in the cairn during the first half of this period, and cremations have also been found at Carronbridge.

The large house with the oven at Lintshie Gutter probably went out of use during the early part of this period for we have a date from charcoal which presumably represents the last charging of the oven. Indeed the settlement seems to have been abandoned, unless the unexcavated platforms contain houses of this or later periods. At Kilpatrick on Arran, a house on a platform like those at Lintshie Gutter and Green Knowe has been dated to this period. Its roof was supported by a sturdy ring of post-holes, like the house on Platform 5 at Lintshie Gutter.

At Temple Wood in the Kilmartin valley the main stone circle was reused for cremation burials at some time between 1500 and 1000. They were not the earliest burials on the site: a body had been placed with a beaker in a cist surrounded by a small kerb cairn just outside the north-eastern edge of the stone circle. Presumably it dates to some time between 2000 and 1500, although it could be earlier. Another inhumation, seemingly of a 6- to 7-year-old child, had been placed in a cist in another kerbed cairn to the east of the circle at some indeterminate date. Now three cremations were placed inside the circle. One was in the corner of a small rectangular setting of slabs. The other two were in neat kerbed cairns. The earlier was at the centre of the stone circle and the later overlapped the central cairn to its northeast. Both had symbolic entrance arrangements on their south-east sides (80).

Cremation burials of this period have also been found on the gravel terraces of the Kilmartin valley, and a small cemetery of kerb cairns at Claggan in Morvern was in use from about the middle of the period. Two out of three small cairns, the largest about 6m (20ft) across and the smallest less than 2.5m (8½ft) broad, both with tall kerbstones, date to before 1000. The third seems to be several centuries later in date. The cairns covered cremations. From this limited evidence it does seem that cremation, often under small kerb cairns, was by now the normal burial ritual in the west.

Just above the cultivated fields at Cul a'Bhaile on the east coast of Jura, a rough drystone wall encloses a peat-covered area of

81 *The house at Cul a'Bhaile, on Jura in western Scotland, shown here during excavation, was initially built with a stone wall capped with earth or turfs, defining an interior about 7.5m (25ft) across. The inner face of the wall was lined by a wattle fence and a ring of posts supported the roof. The entrance was in the south-east and covered by a porch.*

about 0.4ha (1 acre), and in it are the remains of a roundhouse (81). Lower down the hill are remains of an extensive settlement of roundhouses, and the one at Cul a'Bhaile was probably part of a pattern of dispersed settlement. The site had a long history of use before the house was built. Traces of ploughing found under it probably go with a period of intensive cultivation on fields manured with cattle litter, which was followed by a reversion to the rough peaty pasture on which the house was

built. The people who lived in the house cultivated this one field, outside which was rough grazing, but soil erosion was severe, and as the climate deteriorated the house was abandoned, after at least six generations of occupation during which the house was twice remodelled.

Changing the landscape

During this period a landscape not unlike that of the recent past was created. In suitable areas large fields were cultivated; elsewhere small enclosures like that at Cul a'Bhaile protected the cultivated area. The irregular fields of the previous periods, scattered with small clearance cairns, seem to have given way to larger fields with regular boundaries, at least in north-east Scotland. They surely imply intensive and wide-scale ploughing in the valleys

111

below. The large-scale introduction of draught animals allows more land to be cultivated, but makes life more arduous for farmers. They have to feed and manage the oxen; and permanent fields require constant weeding. Much of their effort must have been spent on agriculture and on maintaining pastures for the draught beasts.

As it got wetter and cooler towards the end of this period, peat could have been kept at bay by careful cultivation even in the wetter west and north of Scotland. However, there is much evidence of soil erosion following cultivation and times must have been hard in the more marginal areas. Our best evidence comes from such areas. Around 1250 the settlement in Achany Glen was abandoned; and before 1000 conditions at Cul a'Bhaile seem to have become unsuitable enough for agriculture that the effort of keeping the soil in good condition was too much for the people who lived there. There is, however, no sign that all the fields in the neighbourhood of Cul a'Bhaile were completely abandoned, and perhaps cultivation continued further downhill.

The lack of large ceremonial and burial monuments suggests that there were no great lords or ladies demanding conspicuous display of their control of the land, but it is likely that there was some form of hierarchy at this time, given the intensification in agriculture in the north-east and presumably the east and south-east. In the west, although there is continued evidence for agriculture, a less intensive system seems to have survived.

Cremation seems to have been the main burial ritual throughout most of Scotland. Many of the cremations seem to have been unaccompanied, but some were still placed in urns not unlike those used in most of the settlements of the period; and the inhumations at Grainfoot in the south-east and Cnip in Lewis show that burial rituals remained diverse. Indeed, burials in eastern Scotland seem to show that pots such as beakers and food vessels were still used after 1500.

CHAPTER EIGHT

A time of swords 1000 to 750 BC

Defended settlements

The story of this period contains much that is old, but also things that are new (**82**). In addition to burnt mounds and undefended platform settlements, the first defended settlements were built. In a departure from previous chapters, I shall concentrate on what was new, for the tale of the old would repeat much already written. But it is important to remember that the changes seen in this period took place in a well-populated and well-organized agricultural landscape, in which peasants laboured for themselves and for local lords. Much of their equipment was made of wood, and one extraordinary result of the dating programme by the National Museum is the discovery that solid wooden wheels found at Blair Drummond, Perthshire belong in this period. The wheels were each made of three pieces of ash-wood and suggest ox carts rather than chariots.

On the coast of the Moray Firth, at Portknockie, occupation started on a small promontory which was soon to be defended by a stockade. Similarly, a settlement of three small roundhouses at Myrehead, near Falkirk, seems to have led on to one defended with a stout stockade at some time after 750. Wheat, barley and rye were found in the roundhouses, and burnt fragments of the bones of cattle, sheep or goats and pigs. Two of the houses seem each to have had a large roasting pit inside and in one of them there were several, indicating that the

house remained in use for a long time (**83**). The cooking method involved dumping of burning wood into a pit with the joint of a large animal, all then covered with turf. One of the pots from the site was broadly similar to a vessel found on the platform settlement at Green Knowe of much the same period. Indeed, one of the pits dug during the previous ten generations at Green Knowe may have been a roasting pit, although no burnt turf was noted in it. Myrehead, then, may be the lowland equivalent of a small platform settlement – the home of a small group of peasant farmers.

At Dryburn Bridge in East Lothian the sequence was the reverse of that at Myrehead, for a stockade enclosed the two earliest houses in what was later to become an undefended settlement. The door of the house near the centre of the enclosure pointed towards the more northerly of two entrances through the defences (**84**) and there is little doubt that they were built at much the same time as each other. The house was exceptionally large and it had an unusual arrangement of posts, suggesting that the porch extended inward to form a half-loft covering up to half of the interior. This half-loft may have been used for storing fodder, but it is conceivable that it provided sleeping-quarters. Nearby was a smaller house of the same design.

The settlement expanded, probably after 750, to fill the enclosure; and then spilt across its line. It may not finally have been abandoned until after the second century AD.

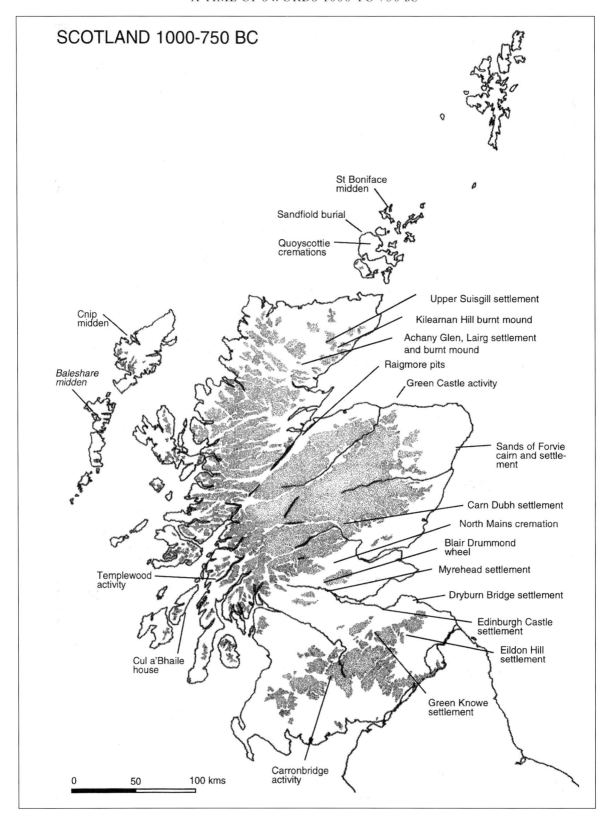

SCOTLAND 1000-750 BC

St Boniface midden

Sandfiold burial

Quoyscottie cremations

Cnip midden

Baleshare midden

Upper Suisgill settlement

Kilearnan Hill burnt mound

Achany Glen, Lairg settlement and burnt mound

Raigmore pits

Green Castle activity

Sands of Forvie cairn and settlement

Carn Dubh settlement

North Mains cremation

Blair Drummond wheel

Myrehead settlement

Dryburn Bridge settlement

Edinburgh Castle settlement

Eildon Hill settlement

Templewood activity

Cul a'Bhaile house

Green Knowe settlement

Carronbridge activity

0   50   100 kms

82 *Sites radiocarbon dated to between 1000 and 750.*

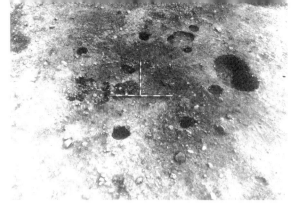

During this long period of occupation ten people were buried here, each in a deep pit. Although the earliest dated burial is somewhat more likely to belong before 750 than after, most of them were contemporary with the later, undefended settlement. Both men and women were buried, their bodies lightly flexed. It may be that these burials reflected earlier traditions, such as those at Grainfoot mentioned in Chapter 7.

Houses dating to between 1000 and 750 have been found on other south-east Scottish sites which were later to become important settlements. A hearth and parts of what may be a house have been excavated on Edinburgh Castle Rock, where in the first and second centuries AD there seems to have been an extensive settlement. Roundhouses on platforms on the slopes of Eildon Hill may have been part of an undefended settlement rather than an early part of the settlement in the great hill-fort occupying the top of the hill, but perhaps it would be wrong to draw too strong a distinction: the change from undefended to defended settlement may reflect social change in fairly

83 *The three roundhouses at Myrehead, in eastern Scotland, were probably between 7 and 12m (23–40ft) across. Although the post-rings of the house shown on this excavation photograph encircled a much smaller area, they would have supported conical roofs with eaves coming down close to the ground. The largest hole visible here was a roasting pit.*

84 *At Dryburn Bridge, in south-eastern Scotland, a stockade was built enclosing an area about 85 by 50m (280 by 165ft). The large house inside it was 18m (60ft) across (it would have been larger in floor-area than many modern houses) and there was a smaller house nearby. There were signs of lightly built structures which may have been animal pens. This artist's impression adds roadways, two haystacks, more pens and some garden patches to what was discovered during excavation.*

static populations, for a pit and a hearth beneath the rampart of the main defensive system also date to this period and imply that people had settled near the top of the hill. Not all was change: occupation continued at the platform settlement at Green Knowe. Higher up the hillside than those of earlier periods, the house of this period was lightly built of slim posts with wattle and daub walls. A small amber bead was found on the platform.

Much as in the previous period the dated sites seem to show farmers practising intensive agriculture in a landscape largely consisting of pastures and ploughed fields with patches of woodland, and bogs and heathy moors. Portknockie, Myrehead, Edinburgh Castle and Eildon Hill were all soon to become defended sites and it is clear that this was a time of change. However, Dryburn Bridge is the only site, of those which can be dated by radiocarbon to this period, which suggests the presence or threat of the warriors who wielded the most characteristic bronze weapons of this period, long swords with their weight concentrated in the lower part of the blade, designed for slashing.

The clearest evidence for bronzeworking comes from undated sites. At Jarlshof, in Shetland, a bronzeworker set up shop in this or early in the next period, and among the fragmentary moulds from the site was one for a sword. A range of tools and ornaments was made in the workshop (**colour plate 12**). Moulds for swords (among other objects) have also been found in the hill-fort on Traprain Law in East Lothian. From there, too, comes a remarkable sign of both continuity and change, a wrought-iron axehead of the same shape as a common type of cast-bronze axehead.

Most weapons, however, have been found in rivers, lochs or boggy areas, like those in the hoard dredged up in 1778 from Duddingston Loch, near Arthur's Seat in Edinburgh (**85**). It seems that here, as elsewhere in Britain and Ireland, there was a cult which involved the throwing of metal offerings into lakes and rivers. The most remarkable example of this practice has been revealed by excavation at Flag Fen near Peterborough in England, where some if not most objects seem to have been made specifically for this purpose. The finds from Duddingston Loch suggest a variant on the practice followed at Flag Fen, for they were found in one concentrated mass. They included a cauldron ring and fragments of spears and swords, and they probably were mostly from a single hoard; but the recorded presence of wooden piles nearby adds spice to the suggestion that the hoard was lobbed into the water from a purpose-built stage.

There is no firm evidence for uniquely Scottish metalworking traditions. Most of the objects found here are of types found in southern Britain or Ireland. The earliest swords are of a type found mostly in eastern and south-eastern England, and in Scotland they have been found mostly in the eastern lowlands. Later types of bronze sword are far more abundant and widespread; unless there was a change in ritual, leading to a higher proportion of them finding their way into rivers and wetlands, they may reflect the growing aggression suggested by the appearance of fortified sites. The hoards in which these later swords are found quite often contain fragments of horse-harness, which taken with the design of the swords suggests that warriors fought from horseback.

Scotland before the Scots

The tale of Scotland before the Scots falls into four parts, and this book deals with the middle two. Hunting and gathering of the produce of the forests and the sea became less important than agriculture about 4000. In the north-east, at least, settlers came direct from the continent. People were buried in chambers under cairns and barrows, except perhaps in the north-east and adjacent areas where their remains were cremated and scattered in sacred enclosures. Slowly the land was cleared and society grew richer and more regional until

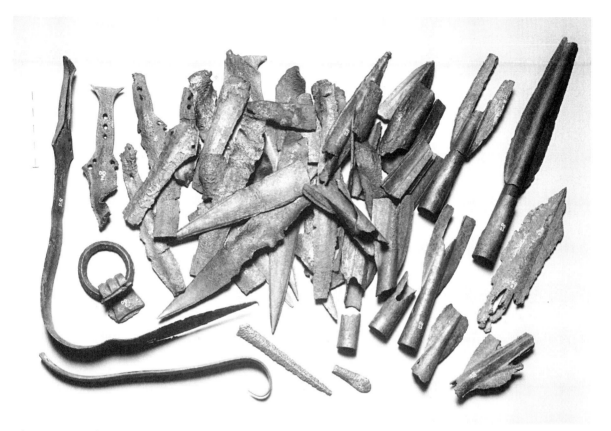

about 3000 when new ideas swept the country. There is some evidence to suggest that they originated in Scotland. Tall stone circles, timber circles and massive ceremonial earthworks were built and a new kind of pottery appeared throughout Britain, along with chieftains who dominated large areas. Stone was quarried and flint was mined. For some unexplained reason this society collapsed after some twenty generations bringing the second part of Scotland's story to an end.

In the vacuum left by the fall of this complex and promising society local groups arose, each selecting from the traditions of the past; in some places these showed much continuity, only pottery styles and the sizes of the ceremonial enclosures changing, but in many places new fashions were adopted, including cults associated with the use of beakers. Around 2000 local metalworking traditions arose in the regions around Inverness; but this seems to have been a false dawn and although there was trade and

85 *The bronze objects dredged up from Duddingston Loch, in south-eastern Scotland, may represent many successive offerings of ritually broken objects, including many spearheads and swords, and a cauldron handle-ring. Only that part of the original find which is preserved in the National Museums of Scotland is shown here.*

exchange with other parts of Britain the people concentrated on breaking in the land. As time went on, the scope for conspicuous display appears to have become increasingly limited. The population grew steadily.

Undefended groups of houses in the uplands and lowlands were probably the common form of settlement throughout the succeeding periods completing the third part of the story. However, from about 750 onwards settlements were increasingly surrounded by fences or banks and ditches. Hill-forts became common, although the defences of some seem to have fallen into disuse between 250 and the end of the

117

millennium. Perhaps even more typical than hill-forts in Scotland as a whole in the period after about 500 are massive roundhouses, predecessors to the dry-stone broch towers of the end of the millennium. They point to a continuation of the changes: petty chieftains and minor lords became increasingly important. There is no need to invoke invaders from Ireland and England to explain this change, nor from the continent, although there is abundant evidence of trade or gift exchange. It is common when herdsmen and peasant farmers live not far from each other for the herdsmen to try to take over by force, creating a petty aristocracy. Alternatively, agricultural intensification of the kind seen in Scotland from 1500 onwards often leads to a change in society. The concept of land ownership becomes more common, or

if not ownership, much closer control of rights to use of the land. If new cultivable land was not available, and if changes in cultivation techniques could not keep pace with a rising population, judging by ethnographic parallels many individuals and families will have become landless labourers. Dominant individuals will have taken advantage of this to exert control over others and to increase their own wealth in land and objects through the surplus they could accumulate.

Whichever of these two social changes best explains what happened, the process was not painless, judging by the swords and spears which characterize the periods after 1000. A new elite began to arise, and as the period covered by this book ended, a new society building great stone houses and forts was about to arise.

Places to visit

Sites

The descriptions of these sites are ordered in a great loop from the northern islands down the east coast, then up the west to the Western Isles.

Shetland: at **Jarlshof (HU398096)** the late Bronze Age houses stand near the beginning of a succession of structures forming a remarkable tour through prehistory. There is a site introduction centre here. The 4500-year-old hall at **Staneydale 'Temple' (HU285502)** is set in a relic landscape full of ancient houses and field walls. The **Shetland Museum** at Lerwick contains many finds from related sites.

Orkney: on the mainland are the 5000-year-old settlements of **Barnhouse (HY308126)** and **Skara Brae (HY231188)**; the latter has a site interpretation centre. Exceptionally fine stone circles in ceremonial enclosures survive: the **Stones of Stenness (HY306126)** and the **Ring of Brodgar (HY294134)**. The tomb at **Maes Howe (HY318128)** is internationally famous and has a site interpretation centre. Barnhouse, the two rings and Maes Howe are all close to each other and, with nearby sites on private land, form the most remarkable combination of tombs, ritual sites and settlement in north-west Europe. Other tombs can be seen at **Unstan (HY283117)**, **Wideford Hill (HY409122)**, **Cuween Hill (HY364128)** and on South Ronaldsay, connected to the main island by road, is **Isbister (ND469843)**, the Tomb of the Eagles. On Rousay at the end of a roll-on roll-off ferry service are fine tombs including **Midhowe (HY429488)**, **Taversoe Tuick (HY426276)**,

Blackhammer **(HY239285)** and **Knowe of Yarso (HY404279)**. The tombs of **The Dwarfie Stone (HY244005)** on Hoy, **Quoyness (HY677378)** on Sanday, **Vinquoy (HY560381)** on Eday and **Holm of Papa Westray South (HY509518)** are more difficult of access, but well worth a visit. The two buildings at **Knap of Howar (HY483519)** on Papa Westray are the earliest visible stone houses in north-west Europe. Kirkwall Museum, in **Tankerness House,** contains displays relating to these sites.

Highland: tombs in Caithness include two cairns at the **Grey Cairns of Camster (ND260441)** and also at **Cnoc Freiceadain (ND013654)**, and one at **Cairn o'Get (ND315411)**. Highland Regional Council has defined a trail nearby, including several cairns, at **Loch of Yarrows**. At the **Hill o' Many Stanes (ND295384)** is a large and remarkable fan-shaped setting of standing stones.

In Glen Urquhart, near Loch Ness, is **Corrimony chambered cairn (NH383303)**, surrounded by a stone circle. The **Clava cairns (NH752439)** are 5 miles east of Inverness. They include two chambered cairns and a ring cairn, each surrounded by a stone circle. **Inverness Museum** has a fine display of prehistoric remains.

Aberdeenshire: There is a motor trail including fine examples of recumbent stone circles such as **Loanhead of Daviot (NJ747288)**, **Easter Aquhorthies (NJ732207)** and **Cullerlie (NJ785042)** – all of which are in the care of Historic Scotland – together with later sites including Pictish symbol stones and hill-forts. The similar monument at **Tomnaverie (NJ486034)** is worth a visit, while **Memsie cairn**

(NJ976620) is just about worth a look from a passing car.

Fife: at **Balfarg (NO280030)** the great 5000-year-old ceremonial enclosure has been laid out for visitors. An excellent guidebook is available from the Council.

Lothian: Cairnpapple (NS987717) has a ceremonial enclosure and cairns of the second millennium BC. The site interpretation centre is likely to remain closed, however.

Dumfries and Galloway: there is a tomb at **Cairn Holy (NX518540)** with an exceptionally fine façade. There are noteworthy rock carvings at **Drumtroddan (NX362447)**, and an alignment of three standing stones. At **Torhouse (NX382565)** there is a low mound edged with standing stones. **Dumfries** and **Kirkcudbright Museums** house displays related to ancient sites.

Arran: the stone circles at **Auchagallon (NR893346)**, **Machrie Moor (NR910324)** and **Moss Farm Road (NR900326)** are worth seeing. They include two tall stone circles and several circles of stubby stones. The fine tombs of **Cairn Ban (NR990262)** and **Torrylin (NR955210)** are also accessible to visitors.

Argyll: Kilmartin valley near Lochgilphead includes the three cairns at **Nether Largie NR830983)** – one with a good carving of axe-heads, and another a chambered cairn – and three others, the **Glebe Cairn, Ri Cruin (NR825971)** and **Dunchraigaig (NR833968)**. In the area around are several rock outcrops with fine carvings, including **Achnabreck (NR856906)**, **Ballygowan (NR816978)**, **Baluachraig (NR831969)**, **Cairnbaan (NR838910)** and **Kilmichael Glassary (NR857934)**. The stone circles at **Temple Wood (NR826978)** are at the heart of this concentration of fine ancient sites. A new visitor centre has recently been opened.

Western Isles: Calanais (NB213330), once known as Callanish, on the west coast of Lewis, is an exceptionally fine stone setting. An avenue of large stones leads to a tall stone circle, inside which is a small chambered tomb. Stone rows point east, south and west. An interpretation centre opened in 1995. The mysterious structure at **Steinacleit (NB396540)** has never been excavated. It may be a prehistoric hall.

Archaeological organizations

Historic Scotland, Longmore House, Salisbury Place, Edinburgh, looks after many of those ancient sites which are easy to visit. Guidebooks, a gazetteer and a map of monuments in its care are available. Members of Friends of Historic Scotland will receive a free gazetteer and map (tel. 0131-668 8600).

For those interested in the records of individual sites throughout Scotland, details are held in the Royal Commission on the Ancient and Historical Monuments of Scotland (RCHMS) in the **National Monuments Record of Scotland**, John Sinclair House, 16 Bernard Terrace, Edinburgh. However, the records are suited more to serious students with a good general knowledge and plenty of time to spare than to casual visitors (tel. 0131-662 1456).

The **National Museums of Scotland** hold a comprehensive collection of ancient artefacts. They are at present housed in premises in Queen Street, Edinburgh; from 1998 they will be kept in a new building in Chambers Street, Edinburgh (tel. 0131-225 7534). Other museums are mentioned above.

The **Council for Scottish Archaeology**, York Buildings, Queen Street, Edinburgh, is an umbrella organization which can provide information on local archaeological societies and groups (tel. as for National Museums).

Further reading

Bell, M. and Walker, M.J.C. *Late Quaternary Environmental Change: Physical and Human Perspectives*, Longman, Harlow and New York 1992. This well-illustrated book gives a wealth of detail and interpretation of environmental changes since the late glacial period, their consequences for people, and the ways in which people have caused environmental changes. Bell and Walker provide a lively account of recent progress in our understanding.

Boserup, E. *The Conditions of Agricultural Growth: The Economics of Agrarian Change under Population Pressure*, Earthscan, London 1993. A classic in the literature of development, and first written in 1965, this may seem an odd recommendation. Yet it provides a wealth of insights into the several different ways in which people respond to growing populations, and how farmers and herders interact with each other. As the preface to the 1993 edition puts it, it delights, enlightens and provokes.

Bradley, R. *Altering the Earth: The Origins of Monuments in Britain and Continental Europe*, Society of Antiquaries of Scotland Monograph Series Number 8, Edinburgh 1993. This book provides in permanent form the 6 Rhind Lectures given to the Society of Antiquaries of Scotland in 1992. Gracefully written and illustrated, and full of stimulating ideas, it provides an insight into how thoughtful modern archaeologists think about the past.

Burl, A. *The Stone Circles of the British Isles*, Yale University Press, New Haven and London 1976. Burl, A. *From Carnac to Callanish: The Prehistoric Stone Rows and Avenues of Britain, Ireland and Brittany*, Yale University Press, New Haven and London 1993. These two books provide a deliciously detailed account of the stone rings and alignments of Scotland in their wider context. These are books to read, to dip into for their lively insights and to take with you on your travels around the country.

Clarke, D.V., Cowie, T.G. and Foxon, A. *Symbols of Power at the time of Stonehenge*, National Museum of Antiquities of Scotland and HMSO, Edinburgh 1985. Particularly for those interested in objects, whether of gold, stone or pottery, this is the most visually exciting modern book about British and Irish prehistory. Its text paints a vigorous picture of the way in which beliefs, skills and everyday life interacted with one another in the past

Davidson, J.L. and Henshall, A.S. *The Chambered Cairns of Orkney*, Edinburgh University Press, 1989. Davidson, J.L. and Henshall, A.S. *The Chambered Cairns of Caithness* Edinburgh University Press, 1991. Henshall, A.S. and Ritchie, J.N.G. *The Chambered Cairns of Sutherland* Edinburgh University Press, 1995. Henshall, A.S. *The Chambered Tombs of Scotland* (2 vols),

Edinburgh 1963 and 1972. Audrey Henshall's book is the classic account of the Neolithic (4000–2500 BC) burial cairns of Scotland; with regional lists and descriptions and also discussion of their forms and contents. The three other books, with her collaborators Jimmy Davidson and Graham Ritchie, are the fruits of new fieldwork.

Parker Pearson, M. *Bronze Age Britain,* English Heritage and Batsford, London 1993. Despite its title, this lively account covers both the Neolithic and the Bronze Age of Britain. With its many reconstruction drawings and its accounts of recent exciting excavations, it gives a lively and accessible account of the changes that took place between 4000 and 900 BC.

Ritchie, A. *Scotland* BC, Historic Scotland, Edinburgh 1996. This authoritative introduction to the prehistoric monuments of Scotland is based around the many fine sites in the care of Historic Scotland. It puts the sites in a broad context so that in travelling through Scotland one can also travel though its deep past.

Wickham-Jones, C. *Scotland's First Settlers*, Batsford/Historic Scotland, London 1994. As well as explaining the way of life of the hunters and gatherers of Scotland, this clear and accessible account tells how archaeologists interpret the past from evidence found in the ground. It explains too how tools and utensils were made at a time when people roamed free through the ancient forests and along the shorelines of Scotland.

Glossary

Archaeological jargon has been avoided as far as possible in this book. Many of the names given to varieties of pottery have also been avoided, although some are so entrenched as to be unavoidable.

agriculture Used here to mean only the growing of crop plants, thus excluding herding or pasturing of animals except when the latter are additionally mentioned.

ard A simple plough.

awl A tool used for piercing leather and similar tasks.

beaker So-called because the Victorians thought that this type of pot was used to hold a drink for the dead. A pot with an S-shaped profile and simple rim, usually highly decorated with impressed or incised patterns, dating between about 2500 and 1500 BC. Fine examples occur on both settlement and burial sites, where they are commonly associated with single inhumations (and occasionally with cremations) in cists (stone coffins); coarse examples are more common in settlements than with burials.

bowl A pot with width greater than its height. Round-bottomed bowls are often the most distinctively shaped and decorated of the pots used by the people who built chambered tombs and farmed before metal came into use.

Bronze Age Commonly used in Britain to refer to the period from about 2500 or 2000 BC to about 750 or 500 BC.

chambered cairn A place for deposition of bodies or skeletons consisting of a chamber under a cairn.

chambered tomb A place for deposition of bodies or skeletons virtually always consisting of a chamber under a barrow or cairn.

clearance cairn A pile of stones cleared from pasture or a field to improve grazing or make agriculture easier.

food vessel So-called because the Victorians thought this type of pot was used to hold food for the dead. A pot usually shaped like a flower pot with a shoulder and a heavy rim. Food vessel bowls and food vessel urns have similar decoration and rim shapes, but different body shapes and sizes. Food vessels are found on settlements, particularly, so far, in the west, and with both inhumations and cremations. Dates vary from about 2500 to 1500 BC.

grooved-ware pot A pot usually shaped like a broad flower pot, often with a simple rim, and commonly decorated with grooves; but also with plastic and incised decoration. Pots of all sizes are known, from coarse containers to fine cups. Dates from about 3000 BC (or earlier) to after 2500 BC.

harrow A farming tool used to prepare a seed bed.

henge An ambiguous term since there are now various definitions, even though it was only recently invented (*c.* 1930). It originally meant a usually large, roughly circular enclosure with an encircling ditch inside a bank pierced by one or two entrances. The term has been extended to include an enclosure with more entrances, with a ditch and no bank, a bank and no ditch, and roughly circular enclosures of all sizes with one or more entrances.

kerb Close-set stones, usually surrounding a cairn or barrow.

kerb cairn A small cairn, often a few metres across, with a relatively massive kerb.

Mesolithic Middle Stone Age, commonly used in Britain to refer to the period from about 10,000 to about 4000 BC, although no remains of human activity in Scotland have yet been reliably dated to before about 7500 BC.

Neolithic New Stone Age, commonly used in Britain to refer to the period from about 4000 to about 2500 or 2000 BC.

network Here used only to mean a set of social or kinship connections.

pastoralism Herding or animal husbandry, thus excluding crop growing except when additionally mentioned.

prehistory Used here to mean the period before writing in Scotland, ending some time between AD 750 and 1000.

ring cairn A roughly circular bank composed of stones. Ring cairns often enclose an area used for cremations.

stone ring This term has been used in preference to the better-known stone circle because the 'circles' are often not truly circular. Stone rings seem often to have had one side 'flattened', or to be oval or elliptical. Such settings are orientated: they are not the same in all directions. The ring at Calanais, for instance, seems to face towards mid-spring and mid-autumn sunrise because its eastern part is flattened or even slightly in-turned.

urn A pot, usually large and often coarsely decorated, with plastic, incised or impressed ornament, dating between about 2000 and 1000 BC. Often found containing cremated human bone, but also found on settlements.

Index

The author
Patrick Ashmore is a Principal Inspector of Ancient Monuments at Historic Scotland and author of numerous articles on a wide range of topics relating to Scottish archaeology.

Titles in the series:

Scotland's First Settlers
Caroline Wickham-Jones
Neolithic and Bronze Age Scotland
P.J. Ashmore
Prehistoric Orkney
Anna Ritchie
Picts, Gaels and Scots
Sally Foster
Viking Scotland
Anna Ritchie
Medieval Scotland
Peter Yeoman
Scottish Abbeys and Priories
Richard Fawcett
Fortress Scotland and the Jacobites
Chris Tabraham and Doreen Grove
Edinburgh Castle
Iain MacIvor
Stirling Castle
Richard Fawcett

Forthcoming:

Celtic Scotland
Ian Armit
Roman Scotland
David Breeze
Industrial Scotland
John Hume
Scottish Castles
Chris Tabraham
Scottish Cathedrals
Richard Fawcett
Scottish Palaces
Denys Pringle
Iona
Anna Ritchie
St Andrews
Richard Fawcett